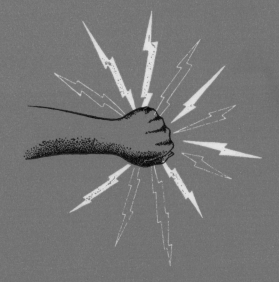

All About Electricity

allabout
books

All About
Electricity

By Ira M. Freeman

Illustrated by Evelyn Urbanowich

RANDOM HOUSE
NEW YORK

Contents

All About Electricity

CHAPTER 1

The
Story of Electricity

Electricity is everywhere in the things around us. It is part of each leaf and stone. It is in the ground we walk on and in the air we breathe. Scientists know that all the things we touch and use are really swirling clouds of electricity, but it took thousands of years to find this out. Only a hundred years ago people thought electricity was something extra that could be added to things or taken away. They did not realize that it was part of all materials.

The electricity that hides in every piece of matter does not usually show itself unless you do something to bring it out. What you do may be something very simple, such as running a comb through your hair!

All About Electricity

Tiny crackling sparks from the comb tell you that electricity is at work. In fact, experiences of this kind were the very first to tell people that electricity exists.

As time passed, scientists and engineers found better ways of coaxing electricity out of materials. They discovered scientific laws about the way electricity acts, and they found hundreds of ways of putting electricity to work. Today we use this great force to light our homes and run our factories. It brings us our favorite radio and television programs. It lets us talk to people halfway around the world. It drives ships and trains, and it guides airplanes through storms and darkness.

From a rubbed comb to the whirring generators in a gigantic power station; from the first crude telegraph line to radio around the earth. This is the story of electricity that you will find in the following pages.

CHAPTER 2

It Started
With Rubbed Amber

More than two thousand years ago, the wise men of ancient Greece took great interest in the things that happen in the world around us. They watched the stars in the sky and the clouds and the rain. They looked at the rocks and rivers and at the waves of the sea. They thought about the different appearances of Nature, and they tried to explain and understand them. Many of their ideas proved to be right and are still true today.

We know that the Greeks of long, long ago were the first to speak of atoms. They were the first people to notice electricity too. What they noticed was very much like what happens when you run a comb through your hair. They found that when a piece of amber was rubbed with cloth or fur it crackled and sparked just like the comb. Besides this, they found that the rubbed amber pulled tiny bits of wood or feathers toward it in a mysterious way. That was all that these wise men discovered, and they had no way of explaining what happened. But it was a start.

For many hundreds of years not much more was learned about electricity. Then, at about the time the Mayflower was getting ready to sail for the New World, English scientists found many other materials that had the same strange pulling power as rubbed amber. They still did not know what caused this power, but they gave it a name. They called it *electricity* after the Greek word for amber. And when any object received electricity by rubbing, they said it received an electrical *charge*.

Meanwhile, other people began to experiment with electricity. A German scientist found a way of making much more electricity than he could get by rubbing a stick of amber. He mounted a large ball of sulfur on a rod and turned it with a crank. When he pressed his hand against the turning ball, great crackling sparks shot out. An English experimenter did the same thing with a hollow glass ball. He rested one hand lightly on

Suddenly the inside of the ball lit up with a bluish glow.

the glass globe and began to turn the crank faster and faster. Suddenly the inside of the ball lit up with a bluish glow. This was probably the first real electric light.

Many years went by before some of the things that seem familiar and simple to us now were discovered. About two hundred years ago, a scientist in France made an important discovery about electricity. You can repeat his experiments very easily after making a simple instrument called an *electroscope*.

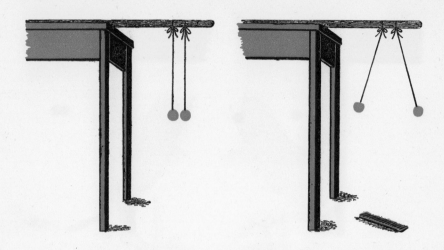

Cut two 6-inch squares of tissue paper, and crumple each into a ball about the size of a marble. Then cover each ball completely with the metal foil from a stick of chewing gum. Lay a broomstick on a table so that it sticks out over the edge. Hang each ball from the stick by a piece of silk thread about a foot long. Slide the threads along the stick until the two balls just touch each other. This setup will be your detector of electricity.

Now run a comb through your hair several times and touch the side of the comb to the two balls. Immediately the two *push each other apart*, and they will stay separated for several minutes. This is important because it shows that in electricity there are forces that push things apart as well as pull things together.

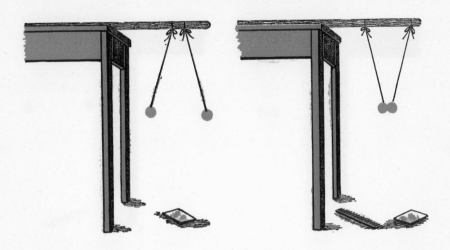

You will have no trouble doing this experiment if you let each ball roll along the side of the comb a little, so that it can pick up enough electrical charge. Do not let either ball touch your finger, or the charge will leak off. And remember that these experiments work best when the weather is dry.

Next touch both balls with your finger to remove all the effects of the last test. Then repeat the experiment. This time, instead of the comb, use a piece of clean glass that has just been rubbed with a silk cloth. Everything works just as before. The two charged balls again push each other apart.

Now the final experiment: Slide the threads a couple of inches apart on the stick. Then charge one ball with the rubbed comb and the other one with the rubbed glass. You will see the two balls pull *toward* each other.

Everything that happened in your experiments can be explained when you know that there are two *opposite* kinds of charge. Our own Benjamin Franklin, who was a scientist and inventor as well as a statesman, made a suggestion. He had the idea of calling the two kinds of charge *plus* (+) and *minus* (−). The kind of electricity on a rubbed glass was named plus, and the kind on amber (or plastic) was named minus. Scientists began to use these names right away, and they are still in use at the present time.

Charges of the same kind push each other apart.
Charges of opposite kinds pull toward each other.

This means that two plus-charged objects will try to shove each other away and so will a pair of minus-charged objects. But a plus and a minus will try to pull closer together.

About two hundred years ago an English scientist had an amusing experience that showed there must be two opposite kinds of electricity. He was in the habit of wearing two pairs of stockings at one time. He put on a white woolen pair for warmth and over these a black silk pair for the sake of appearance. He would take off both stockings together from one foot. Then, when he pulled the woolen one out from inside the silk one, he noticed that both of them magically rounded out to the shape of a foot. The two black stockings began to push each other away, even when quite far apart. So did the two white stockings. They jumped around almost as if alive. But the black and white would cling together and flatten out. When he pulled them apart, they would once more round out like blown-up balloons. This could be done again and again until the charge had all leaked away.

A plus charge and a minus charge are attracted to each other.

CHAPTER 3

Atoms Are
Made of Electricity

The push-pull rule for electric charges cleared up many things that had puzzled scientists, but they wanted to know more. They wondered what *really* went on when things became charged. It took a long time to work this out, and the results have become clear only in the last fifty years or so.

The surprising thing is that in order to understand electricity, we have to understand something about what ordinary materials are made of. Every bit of matter in our surroundings—even the smoothest, hardest and most solid-looking piece—is really made of separate tiny bits of matter called *atoms*. If you could enlarge a steel sewing needle until it was a hundred miles long, you would no longer see a piece of "solid" steel. Instead, the needle would be a swarm of tiny, jiggling atoms. Atoms are actually far, far too small to be seen, but there are clever ways of showing that they really exist. They can even be weighed and measured and counted.

A single atom is about a hundred millionth of an inch across. Atoms of different kinds usually clump together in small groups. Each group is called a *molecule*. Even these molecules are unbelievably small. If all the mole-

New York City

Philadelphia

If you could enlarge a needle to stretch from New York to Philadelphia, you could see the separate atoms.

cules in one drop of water were lined up side by side, the row would reach from the earth to the sun, 93 million miles away!

All the different kinds of matter in the universe are made up of molecules of various kinds. Each kind is a different combination of atoms.

Until about fifty years ago, the atom seemed to be the smallest bit of anything that could exist. Then came a discovery that showed that atoms are made of even smaller things. Experimenters found a way to pull little particles out of atoms. These particles are nearly 2,000 times lighter than even the smallest atom, and it takes about 30 billion billion billion of them to weigh an ounce. Each of these particles carries a certain tiny amount of minus electricity, and so the particles were called *electrons*. No matter what kind of atoms the electrons come from, they always turn out to be *exactly alike*.

Now the scientists were really puzzled. They knew that if an ordinary piece of matter had only a minus charge, it would pull small things toward it as a rubbed comb does. They figured that there must be *something else* in each atom that had a plus charge. Surely enough, after years of searching, plus-charged particles were finally found in all atoms. They were named *protons*. A proton carries exactly as much plus charge as an electron carries minus charge. And a proton is 1,836 times as heavy as an electron.

After much more work, scientists found that atoms contain a third kind of particle. They called it a *neutron* because it is electrically *neutral*, which means that it has no charge. A neutron is just about as heavy as a proton.

Every atom in the world is made of just these three things—electrons, protons and neutrons. That is why we can truly say that *everything* has electricity in it.

Modern science can now tell us how the particles are arranged in atoms. The "heavy" particles (the protons and neutrons) are in a tight cluster at the center of the atom. This cluster is called the *nucleus*.

Different kinds of atoms have different numbers of protons and neutrons in the nucleus. For example, coal is made up mainly of carbon atoms. The nucleus of a carbon atom contains 6 protons and 6 neutrons. An atom of iron has 26 protons and 30 neutrons in its nucleus. A radium atom's nucleus is built of 88 protons and 138 neutrons.

But the electrons do not like company. They always stay far away from the nucleus. In fact, if you imagine the nucleus of an atom magnified until it is as big as a bunch of grapes, the electrons would be marbles roaming around as far as several miles away. So you see that an atom is mostly empty space, with the heavy nucleus at the middle and the electrons swarming around the outside. And in every case, there are just as many of the outer electrons as there are protons in the nucleus. This keeps the charge balanced, so that the whole atom is electrically neutral.

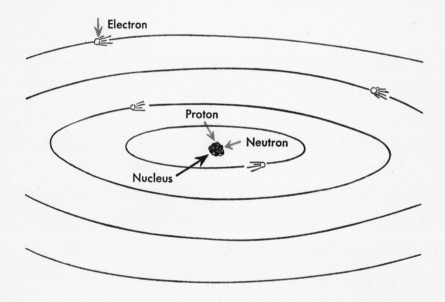

Electrons always stay far away from the nucleus.

CHAPTER 4

Electricity on the Move

Whenever you give a charge to an object by rubbing, or in any other way, you do not really "produce" any electricity. All you do is spoil the evenness of the mixture of plus and minus that was there at the start.

When two different materials, such as plastic and wool, are rubbed together, the rubbing gives their atoms a good chance to get close to each other. Some electrons come loose from the atoms of the wool and stick to the atoms of the plastic. That gives the plastic a *minus* charge because electrons have this kind of charge. The wool, which was neutral to begin with, is now short this much minus charge, leaving it with a *plus* charge.

In solid materials it is always the electrons that move

across from one object to the other. The protons and neutrons are down deep in the atoms, and they stay where they are. Any object that has less than its usual number of electrons is plus-charged, and one that has more than its usual number is minus-charged.

The experimenters back in the early days found that a charge would spread easily over some materials, especially metals, but would stay in place on other materials such as glass or hard rubber. The materials that let the charge move easily are called electrical *conductors* and the others are called *insulators*.

When you touched a rubbed comb to the metal-

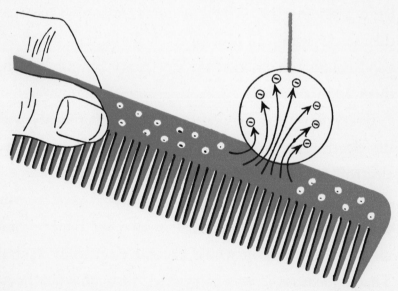

Electrons running off the comb spread out over the whole ball.

covered ball of your electroscope, the electrons that ran off the comb spread out over the whole ball. Each one tried to get as far away from the others as possible. But while the electrons were still on the comb they stayed in place, because the comb is made of an insulator. Electrons cannot move very much along an insulator. That is why you had to roll the ball along the comb to transfer enough charge.

Insulators are used when we want to keep a charge in one place. The electroscope ball was hung from a silk thread. Silk is an insulator and so it did not let the charge leave the ball. Electric power lines hang from large glass insulators for the same reason. The wires themselves are made of copper or aluminum, which are good conductors, so that the electricity can move along them easily.

Everything that happened in your experiments with the electroscope can be explained when you know that electrons can go from one material to another.

No matter which kind of charge you gave to your electroscope, touching the ball with your finger would make it "go dead." It would become electrically neutral. That is because it was connected, through your body, to the earth. Electricians call this a *ground* connection.

All About Electricity

The earth is such an enormous storehouse of charge that it can easily take on or give up enough electrons to neutralize the charge on any object.

If you scuff your feet on a wool rug and bring your finger near a metal doorknob, there will be a tiny spark, and you will feel a little stinging shock. Electrons that gathered on your body when you shuffled across the carpet jumped through the air to the doorknob and then leaked off to the ground. The tires of a car, rubbing on the road, build up a charge on the body of the automobile. Hanging a conducting strip from the axle lets the charge leak off to the road.

Benjamin Franklin wondered whether a flash of lightning was just a giant spark of electricity. He decided to test this idea by flying a kite into the clouds during a thunderstorm. He made his kite by stretching a large handkerchief over a pair of crossed sticks. One stormy day he sent the kite up on the end of a cotton string. At the lower end of the string he hung a metal key. Then he tied a short piece of silk thread to the string so his hand would not touch it directly. He must have been very nervous as he realized that, if his idea proved correct, this silk thread was all that insulated his body from a dangerous electrical charge.

As Franklin's finger approached the key, a spark jumped across.

As soon as the string was wet it became a conductor, ready to lead any electricity down that might be in the clouds. Hesitantly, Franklin brought his finger close to the key. With a crackling sound, a spark jumped across. Now he knew that lightning and electricity were the same thing.

Franklin went on to invent the lightning rod for protecting houses from damage by lightning. To understand how a lightning rod works, you will need to see

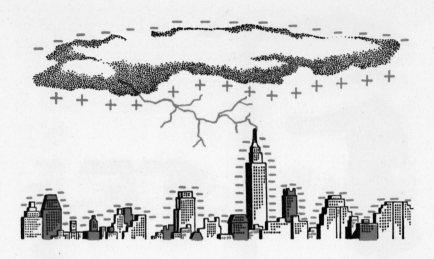

Sometimes lightning will jump from a cloud to a tall building.

what modern science says about lightning itself. The charge is produced when tiny drops of water in the clouds rub against the air. For some reason, the bigger drops get plus charges and the smaller ones get minus charges.

The larger drops settle to the bottom of a cloud. After enough charge has separated out, the air is no longer able to insulate the two kinds and there is a tremendous spark, which is lightning. Most of the flashes are from one part of a cloud to another and do no harm, but about one in every ten will strike over to the earth. The flash usually jumps to a high place, such as a tree or the roof of a house, where it may do great damage.

A lightning rod is a pointed metal bar mounted on top of a house. It is connected by a heavy wire to a sheet of metal buried in the ground. Suppose a storm cloud comes overhead. The plus charge in the lower layers of the cloud pulls electrons up from the earth through the wire. The electrons leak off from the sharp point and neutralize the charge on the cloud before it can build up and become dangerous. Even if there is a flash, the electricity goes through the wire instead of through the house itself, and no damage is done.

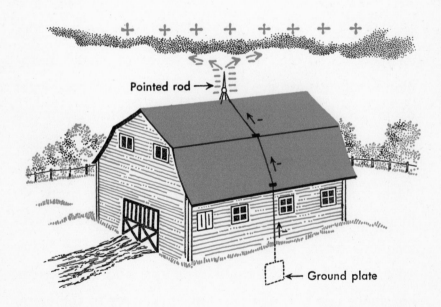

Electricity goes through the wire instead of through the barn.

CHAPTER 5

The
Current Goes 'Round

As long as an electric charge stays in place on an object, you hardly know it is there. But when it moves from one place to another, it shows up by making a spark or producing heat, or by doing other things. Like a horse or a tractor, electricity does some work for us only when it is moving.

In an electric spark, there is a movement of charge for just an instant and then nothing more happens. In order to keep electricity moving steadily, you need something that will keep piling it up. The crude electrical machines described on page 6 can do this. An electric *battery*, such as the one in your flashlight, does it much better.

The invention of the electric battery came as a result of some experiments on frogs' legs. The time was about two hundred years ago. The place was the laboratory of an Italian doctor named Luigi Galvani. Dr. Galvani and his helper were working on the body of a dead frog. Near by another experimenter was running an electrical machine. The doctor noticed that whenever the machine sparked, the frog's leg would twitch. Electricity could make a dead frog move!

Galvani decided to see if the electricity that Franklin had taken from the clouds could do the same thing. One day he took several frogs' legs out onto a balcony, getting ready to test them with electricity from his lightning rod. He hung them on the iron railing by means

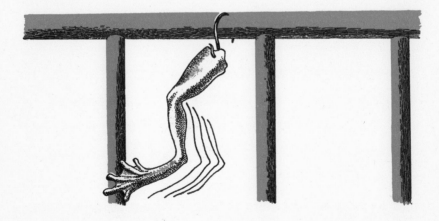

The frog's leg jerked as if electricity had touched it.

of copper hooks. The wind happened to blow one of the legs against the bars of the railing. Each time it touched, the leg jerked as if electricity passed through it. Dr. Galvani was puzzled. No charge had been drawn from the clouds, but the frog's leg twitched just the same! Where did the electricity come from? Galvani thought that some kind of "animal electricity" made the leg move.

Another Italian scientist, Alessandro Volta, made some experiments of his own. He knew that the twitching took place only when the frog's leg was touched with two *different* conducting materials such as iron and copper, or tin and carbon. He realized that the leg itself was only a kind of electric meter that showed when electricity was moving. Otherwise it was not needed at all.

Volta built a stack of zinc and copper disks separated by pieces of paper soaked in salt water. It worked perfectly, giving the same effect as the electrical machines you already know about; but it was much steadier and could be used again and again before it would wear down. Volta also made a "crown of cups" using a set of jars filled with salt water joined by strips of two dif-

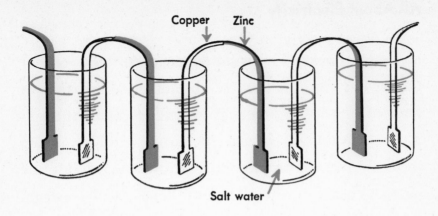

Copper Zinc

Salt water

Each jar is called a cell, the whole set a battery.

ferent metals. Each jar was called a *cell*, and the whole set made up the first true electric *battery*.

Batteries were improved as time went on. For over a hundred years they were the only really dependable way to make electric charges move. Today's very efficient batteries are necessary as sources of electricity for flashlights and portable radios. And it all started with the twitching of a frog's leg.

When Volta put together his stack of metal disks, he not only invented the electric battery but he also discovered electric currents. *An electric current is a stream of moving charges.* In a conductor such as a wire, the things that move are the electrons. So the current in a wire is a swarm of electrons moving through the metal. The loose electrons are forced along through the spaces between the atoms. The rubbing and bumping that takes place as they go forward produces heat in the wire. If the wire is quite thin, it may get red hot like the wire in a toaster or electric heater. A very fine wire, like the *filament* of an electric light bulb, glows white hot when the current flows. The filament would burn up in a moment if it were not sealed into the bulb where the air cannot get at it.

In many ways electricity acts like water. For instance, we say that electric charges flow from one place to another. Also, electricity—like water—cannot be compressed into a smaller space. The electrons in a wire cannot be forced any closer together because they all have the same kind of charge and so must push away from each other.

Suppose you pour water into one side of a tall U-shaped tube like the one in the picture. As the water gets deeper, it pushes harder and harder on the closed valve at the bottom of the tank. Now open the valve. Pressure makes the water rush through to the right. The flow stops only when the level of water becomes the same on the two sides and there is no difference in pressure. There was a *current* of water only while there was a *difference of pressure* on the two sides.

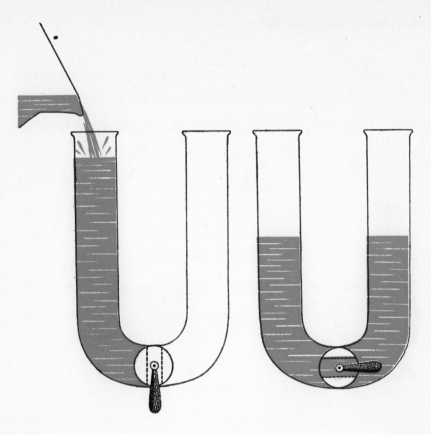

With equal pressure on both sides, the water stops flowing.

In the same way there can be a current of electricity only if there is a difference of "electrical pressure" between two places. In electricity instead of saying pressure, we say *potential*. Electrons flow from a rubbed comb to a metal ball because the comb and the ball are at different potentials. As soon as the two become equal, the flow stops. Notice that this is exactly like the action of the water in the U-shaped tube.

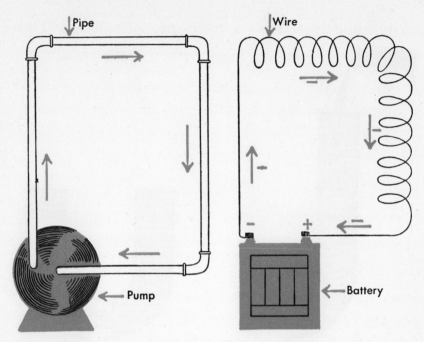

Pipe

Wire

Pump

Battery

Like a pump, a battery keeps current flowing.

To make electricity useful, the current must keep on flowing. If you wanted to make a water system where there would be a lasting current, you could hook up a pump and a loop of pipe as in the picture. The pump keeps up a difference of pressure between its outlet and its return connection, and this sends the water around the loop again and again.

In the same way you can hook up a loop of wire to the two posts (or *terminals*) of a battery, which is a kind of electrical pump. A battery does not "make electricity" any more than a pump produces water. The battery only moves the loose electrons that are always in the wire.

Chemical action in the cells takes electrons from one terminal and puts them on the other one. The electrons always tend to get back the way they were; and if a loop of wire is connected between the two posts, electrons flow through it from the minus terminal to the plus one. Then, these electrons are carried on through the cells and keep moving around the loop again and again, as long as the chemicals keep up a difference in potential across the battery.

So you see that two things are needed in order to have a lasting electric current. We must have something that keeps up a difference in potential, such as a battery; and there must be a complete path or loop, called a *circuit*. Then we can really put electricity to work.

Electricians must know how to measure the things that happen in a circuit. To see how they do this, take another look at the water pipe system. If you connect a pressure gauge across the pump, it tells you the difference of pressure between the outlet and return pipes. Then, to find out how much water is being forced through the pipe each second, you would cut the pipe

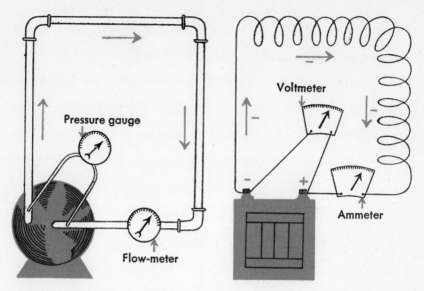

The voltmeter measures potential, the ammeter measures current.

at some point and connect a *flow-meter* right into the circuit. This meter tells how many gallons pass through the pipe each second.

In an electric circuit, the same thing is done. A special meter is connected across the battery, or across any two points in the circuit whose difference of potential you wish to know. The measure of electrical potential is the *volt*, named for Alessandro Volta, and the meter is called a *voltmeter*. As an example, the potential difference across the posts of a flashlight cell is about 1.5 volts. Across the wires of a house lighting circuit the "voltage" is 115 to 120 volts. In a thunderstorm, there may be billion-volt flashes of lightning!

The current in a circuit is measured in *amperes*, named after the French scientist André Ampère who lived 150 years ago. The instrument is called an *ammeter*. When a current of one ampere flows in a wire, it means that more than six billion billion electrons pass each point of the wire every second. A 60-watt lamp in your house carries a current of about half an ampere. The currents that work your telephone are about one ten-thousandth of an ampere, but in a lightning stroke, the current may be as much as half a million amperes.

Water will flow more easily through a short, wide pipe than through a long, narrow one. Exactly the same thing is true in an electric circuit. If you connect a long, thin wire to the terminals of a battery, the current will be weak. But if you use a short, thick wire, the current will be strong. The kind of wire you choose will make a difference too. You find that a copper wire will let more current flow than will an iron wire of the same size.

The action of a wire in holding back a current is called *resistance*. The exact way to measure the resistance of a wire was worked out by a German scientist,

G. S. Ohm. Ohm found that the current on a circuit depended on how big he made the battery voltage and how small he could make the resistance. The measure of resistance was later named after this scientist. If a potential difference of one volt is put across a wire having one *ohm* resistance, the current that flows will be just one ampere. The resistance of the heating coil of an electric toaster may be 20 ohms. The filament of a 60-watt lamp has a resistance of about 200 ohms.

CHAPTER 6

Magnets

If you have a toy magnet, you know that it will pick up tacks or paper clips. A compass is also a magnet. You can use the toy magnet to make the compass needle swing one way or the other, depending on which end of the magnet you bring near.

Facts such as these were noticed thousands of years ago. People found that a sliver of a certain kind of rock was a ready-made magnet. It would set itself north and south when allowed to turn freely. They used compasses made in this way to guide them in their travels, but they had no understanding of what magnets were.

A toy magnet makes the compass needle swing aside.

Some experimenters claimed that a magnet would lose its power when rubbed with garlic and become stronger when smeared with goat's blood!

These days it is very easy to find out the true facts about magnets. For example, you lay a straight magnet on a pile of tacks, and when you pick up the magnet you find that the tacks stick to it mostly near the two ends. These two places, one near each end of the magnet, are called its *poles*. If you hang up the magnet by a thread and use it as a compass, one of these poles swings toward the north. This is called the north pole, or N-pole of the magnet. The other one is the south, or S-pole.

Every ordinary magnet has these two opposite poles.

It reminds you of the two opposite kinds of electricity, plus and minus, but there is a difference. You know that you can put either a plus or a minus charge of electricity on any object. However, you can never have just one kind of pole all by itself on a magnet. If you cut a magnet in two, new poles appear near the cut ends and again you have two complete magnets.

If you experiment with two magnets, you discover a push-pull rule just like the one for electrical charges given on page 10.

Poles of the same kind push each other apart.

Poles of opposite kind pull toward each other.

This says that two N-poles will try to shove each other away and so will a pair of S-poles. But an N and an S

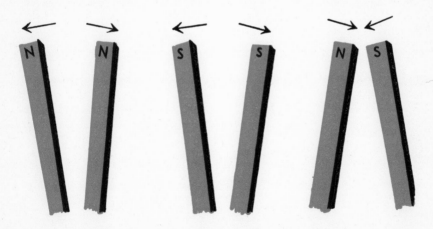

Poles of the same kind push each other apart.

will try to pull closer together. If you have two straight magnets, or one magnet and a compass, you can test this yourself.

It is puzzling to watch two magnet poles or two electric charges push or pull each other even though they are not joined in any way we can see. Scientists have not been able to find any real reason for these forces. It is something which we must take for granted, just as we do not question the earth's gravity, which pulls everything toward the center of the earth.

One of the greatest scientists who ever lived showed that there is a way of picturing the pushes and pulls of electric charges or magnet poles. His name was Michael Faraday, and he lived in England about a hundred years ago. As a boy, Faraday worked for a bookbinder. He became interested in science by looking at some of the books in the shop. Through hard work and study he finally became a first-class scientist and made many important discoveries, especially in electricity and chemistry.

In order to picture in his mind what happens when one magnet pole pushes or pulls on another, Faraday imagined little threads going out from N-poles and ending up on S-poles. He called these make-believe threads

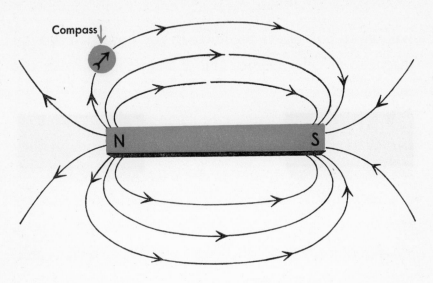

Faraday imagined lines of force going from N-poles to S-poles.

lines of force. Near a straight magnet, the lines of force look like the ones shown in the picture. They all start out from the N-pole, then curve around and come back to the S-pole. If you put a small compass down anywhere near such a magnet, the compass needle will set itself right along the line of force at that place.

Faraday went even further. In order to explain the push-pull rule, he supposed that the lines of force can be stretched like rubber bands. Besides this, each line tries to push its neighbors sideways. The upper drawing on the next page shows the lines of force between the two *opposite* magnet poles. Notice how the lines stretch across from one pole to the other, as if trying to pull the

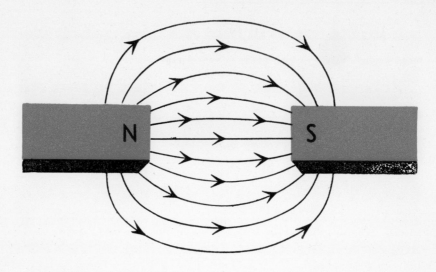

Imaginary lines of force pull opposite poles together.

two toward each other. The lower picture on this page shows the lines between two poles of the *same* kind. This time, instead of going across, the lines coming out of each

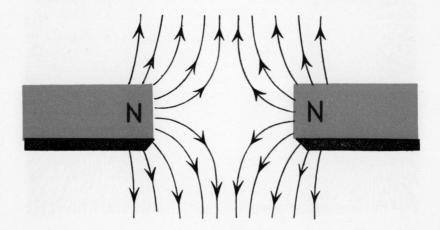

Here, the lines of force are pushing two similar poles apart.

pole seem to turn away from each other, pushing side-ways and forcing the two poles apart.

Remember that these lines of force are no more real than the lines of latitude or longitude on a map. But they are very useful for keeping in mind what happens.

There is a way of mapping out magnetic lines of force. All you need do is to put the magnet on a table and lay a card over it. Then scatter some tiny bits of iron (iron filings) all over the card. Tap it with a pen-cil, and the filings will line up to give a very real-look-ing picture of the lines of force.

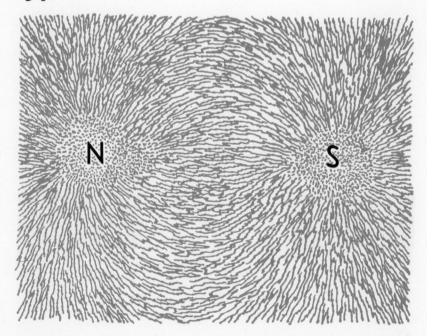

Iron filings on a card are lined up by the magnet underneath.

CHAPTER 7

Electromagnets

As scientists found out more and more about magnetism, they began to wonder if, in some way, magnetism and electricity were really two forms of the same thing. However, a few differences worried them. A single kind of charge can be put on an object, but a magnet can never have just one pole. Besides, any object will take a charge of electricity but magnets can be made of only a few materials, such as iron. There are other differences too. Even so, many people believed that there must be *some* connection between electricity and magnetism if only they could find it.

The missing piece in the puzzle was found by a Danish science teacher, Hans Christian Oersted. The year was 1819. Professor Oersted had been experimenting with an electric battery. In his hand he held a wire connected to the battery. He was about to disconnect the wire when something made him stop. "I wonder what would happen," he said to himself, "if I put the wire near this compass needle." Carefully, he brought the wire closer and held it just above the needle.

Oersted himself did not know what to expect, but what did happen must have surprised him. The compass needle did not try to move toward the wire, or away from it either. Instead it *turned* and pointed almost east! "Why east?" thought Professor Oersted. "Suppose I

The electric current made the compass needle swing aside.

connect the wire so that the current goes in the opposite direction." When this was done, the needle immediately swung to the other side, pointing west. When the
battery was disconnected, the needle went back to its
original north-south position and everything stopped.

Oersted had solved the problem. There is a relation
between electricity and magnetism, but it is not the kind
people expected to find. They were looking for some
connection between magnetism and electric *charges*.
The real story is that we get magnetism only when
charges move. This means there must be an electric *current*. And the queer thing about the magnetic force is
that instead of being straight toward or away from the
wire that carries the current, it is crossways.

Everywhere, people began experimenting with magnets and currents. In France, Ampère made a coil by
winding a long wire in the shape of a spiral. He saw
that this would bring more wire near the compass
needle, and so would make the force stronger. When
the current is turned on, a coil of this kind acts just like
a straight magnet. It has the same kind of lines of force
around it. It has a north pole near one end and a south
pole near the other. If you hang the coil by a thread, it

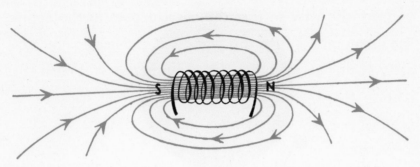

In an electromagnet, the wire is coiled into a spiral.

swings into a north-south position just like a steel magnet. Such a coil is called an *electromagnet*.

By winding the wire on an iron rod, the electromagnet can be made more than a thousand times stronger. The lines of force seem to go through iron more easily than through the air. You will find that electromagnets are used in all sorts of electrical instruments and machines, from automobile horns to cyclotrons. They are useful because they can be made stronger than any regular magnet, and also because their strength can be changed simply by changing the current that flows in the wire. And they can be "turned off" altogether by stopping the current. When the current is shut off, the electromagnet is once more just a coil of wire. It no longer acts like a magnet at all.

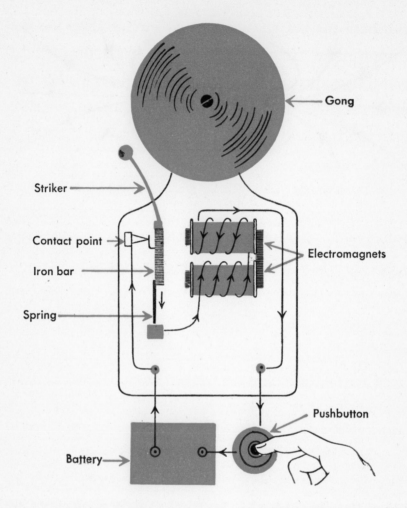

Gong

Striker

Contact point

Iron bar

Spring

Electromagnets

Pushbutton

Battery

As the coils become magnetized, the striker hits the gong.

One of the simplest uses of the electromagnet is in an electric buzzer or doorbell. Usually there is a pair of electromagnets wound with many turns of thin wire. The picture shows how everything is hooked up. When you push the button, it closes the circuit. This lets the current flow from the battery through the contact point, then through the coils and back to the other terminal of the battery. The coils become magnetized, pulling the iron bar to the right and making the striker hit the gong.

As soon as the bar starts to move toward the magnets, it no longer touches the contact and the current stops. But with no current in them the coils are no longer magnets. They let the bar go, and a spring pulls it back to the left. Once more the circuit is closed, and everything repeats. As a result, the striker taps the bell many times a second.

Even in these days of telephones, radio and television, the telegraph is still a very important way of sending information quickly from one place to another. Electromagnets are the main part of any telegraph system. Within a few years after Oersted's discovery, many inventors came out with ideas for sending messages by electricity. Ampère himself made a telegraph using small electromagnets at the end of twenty-six wires, one for each letter of the alphabet. Like most of the other systems that were suggested, this was too complicated. Morse found a way of using just a single wire. In 1844, after

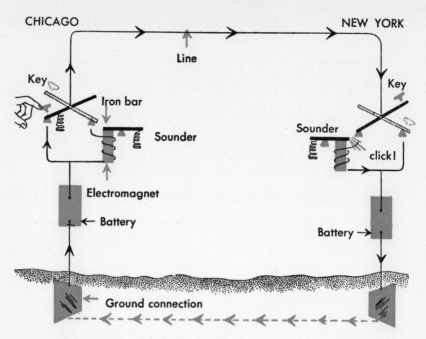

CHICAGO · NEW YORK · Line · Key · Iron bar · Sounder · Electromagnet · Battery · Key · Sounder · click! · Battery · Ground connection

This is the setup of a simple telegraph system.

much experimenting, he was able to open the first commercial line, running forty miles between Washington and Baltimore.

The picture will help you understand how a simple telegraph works. This is not a picture of an actual telegraph system, but only a diagram showing how the main parts are connected. The *key* at either station is simply a switch that closes the circuit for a moment when it is pressed down. Otherwise, a spring holds it in the open position. The *sounder* uses an electromagnet. When current flows in the windings, the iron bar is pulled down against the magnet, making a loud click.

When the operator at Chicago taps his key, the current flows as the arrows show, going out over the line and working the sounder at the New York station. The current comes back through the earth itself, so that only one wire is needed to make the complete circuit.

Quick taps of the key are "dots" and longer taps are "dashes." There is a code made up of certain combinations of dots and dashes to stand for the letters of the alphabet and for numbers. The operator can "read" the message by listening to the clicks. There are ways, too, of making a machine print the dot-and-dash message on a paper tape. In the *teletype* system there is a special electric typewriter at each end of the line. As the message is typed at the sending end, the machine prints it out at the receiving end.

CHAPTER 8

Meters and Motors

Electromagnets help us to measure electric currents and voltages because they are used in making ammeters and voltmeters. The most common kind of electrical meter has a coil that can turn on an axle, as in the picture. The coil is between the poles of a large U-shaped steel magnet. Suppose the instrument is an ammeter. Then the current to be measured is run right through the windings of the coil. When the current is on, the coil becomes an electromagnet, with an N-pole near one end and an S-pole near the other. The N-pole of the steel magnet pushes the N-pole of the coil away, and the S-pole of the magnet pushes the S-pole of the coil away. This makes the coil turn in the direction of the arrow. The pointer then shows the amount of current or the voltage.

There are many other uses for electromagnets besides the ones already mentioned. They are used in all sorts of signaling devices. They are used as lifting magnets which can pick up tons of scrap iron or steel rails. The world's biggest magnets are used in the giant machines that scientists build for studying atoms. The newest and

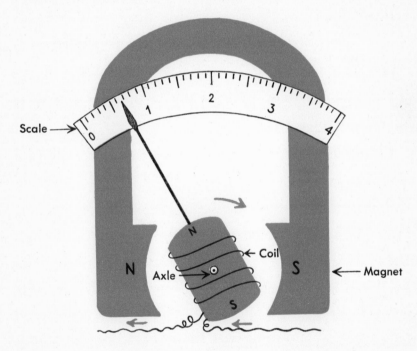

When the current flows, the coil turns and moves the pointer.

largest "atom-smasher" has a tremendous oval magnet 700 feet long, which is big enough to hold two football fields!

But as far as general usefulness goes, the most important work that electromagnets do is in electric *motors*. This kind of motor is really a machine that changes the power of an electric current into the power of motion. Then this motion can be used to turn other machines that do many kinds of work for us.

It is hard to say just when the first motor was invented. The swinging compass needle in Oersted's experiment was, in a way, an electric motor. But much more had to be done to get a practical motor powerful enough to run machinery.

The simplest kind of motor has a coil that is wound on an iron rod. The coil and rod together form the *armature* of the motor. The armature turns on an axle between the poles of a metal magnet, called the *field magnet*, which stands still. The whole thing is very much like the arrangement used in an ammeter or voltmeter, except for one thing. In a meter the coil can turn only a given amount against the twist of a spring. In a motor the armature is arranged to keep on turning in

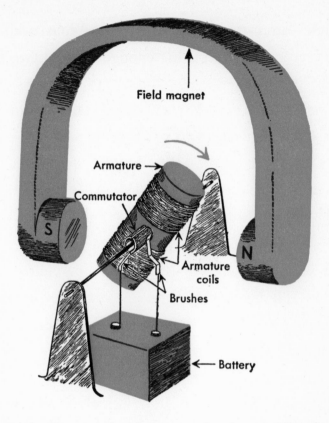

Field magnet

Armature

Commutator

S

N

Armature
coils

Brushes

Battery

In a motor, the armature keeps turning in one direction.

one direction. This is made possible by a sort of automatic switching arrangement called a *commutator*.

The picture will help you to see how a simple motor is built. Current from a battery is led into the armature coil by means of two strips of metal, called *brushes*, that press against opposite sides of the commutator. The commutator is a metal ring mounted on the armature. The ring has been cut in half, and one end of the armature coil is connected to each part, as the sketch shows.

Suppose the current flows in the armature coil in such a way that the upper end is an S-pole and the other end an N-pole. The upper end of the armature will be attracted by the N-pole of the field magnet and at the same time pushed away by the S-pole. This makes the armature turn in the direction of the arrow.

Now when the armature poles get right opposite the poles of the field magnet, you might expect that everything would stop. But it does not, and this is where the commutator comes in. When the motor turns just a little farther, the brushes slide over onto the opposite halves of the commutator. This makes the current go the opposite way in the armature coil and the N-pole now becomes an S-pole, and the S-pole becomes an N-pole. The armature *keeps turning in the direction of the arrow* as before, because the ends that were pulled toward the poles of the field magnet are now being pushed away. The commutator is always ready to switch over the current at the right instant, and the armature keeps turning in one direction, which is what we want.

This is the simplest form of electric motor. You can

get a kit for building such a motor in any toy store or hobby shop. Putting together one of these models is the best way to understand just how such a machine works.

Although your toy motor will work fairly well, its movement cannot be very smooth, and it will just about keep itself going. A practical motor that can drive other machines must be made a little differently. The field magnet of a real motor is not a steel magnet. Instead, it is a strong electromagnet that gets its current from the battery. In place of only two poles, it may have several, spaced all around the frame of the motor. A practical motor usually has a large number of armature coils wound into slots spaced around the edge of the armature. Instead of having only two parts, the commutator

Electric motors drive this aircraft carrier.

has many. These changes make the machine operate smoothly and give it much more turning power.

The first really practical electric motor was built only a little more than a hundred years ago. Today, motors of many kinds and sizes are doing useful work everywhere. There are many motors in your home, from the tiny one in the electric clock to the larger ones that run the electric fan, the vacuum sweeper, the refrigerator and the washing machine. A motor starts the engine of your car. Elevators and even some ships and trains are driven by electric motors.

There may be more than fifty electric motors on an airplane, pumping fuel to the engines, changing the pitch of the propellers, moving the control surfaces, and so on. The set of motors in a steel-rolling mill may have the power of more than 10,000 horses. One motor recently built to run a water-pumping station is rated 65,000 horsepower.

Hans Christian Oersted lived at the same time as another famous Dane, Hans Christian Andersen. But Oersted's discovery of how an electric current can make magnetism led to much more wonderful things than you will find in any of Andersen's fairy tales.

CHAPTER 9

Generators—
Better Than Batteries

Although Oersted's discovery showed scientists and engineers how to put electricity to work, something else was needed. Up to that time, the only practical way to produce an electric current was to use batteries. But batteries were not enough if people wanted to use large motors. A battery is expensive and lasts only until the chemicals in it are used up. What was needed was some way of obtaining electric current in any amount. Until this was discovered, electromagnets and motors could be nothing more than interesting toys, and even electric lighting could not come into general use.

After Oersted had shown that an electric current could produce magnetism, some experimenters wondered if the opposite thing could also be done. *Was it possible to obtain an electric current by using magnetism?*

Many scientists worked on this problem, and in 1831 two people reached an answer almost at the same time. One of these scientists was Michael Faraday. The other was Joseph Henry, an American. They lived thousands of miles apart, one in England and the other in the new country of America; but their lives were alike in many ways. Each came from a poor family, and each began to earn his own living while still a boy. Faraday worked for a bookbinder and Henry for a watchmaker. Both boys first became interested in science when they happened to read books on this subject. And each, after years of hard study, became a great scientist and the head of a large scientific research institution in his own country.

Faraday connected a wire to a meter. Then he placed a steel magnet near the wire. Although he probably expected an electric current to flow in the wire, nothing happened. Then he changed the arrangement. In place of the single wire, he used a coil of insulated wire wound on a paper tube. And instead of just laying the magnet down near by, he shoved one end of it into the coil. You can imagine his feeling of joy when the needle of the meter jerked to one side for an instant. This meant that the magnet had made a current flow. A current had been produced without any batteries!

Excitedly Faraday jerked the magnet out of the coil again. Once more the meter showed a sudden "kick" of current, this time in the opposite direction. As long as the magnet was held still, nothing happened. There was a current only while the magnet *moved*. That was the whole secret. Everybody had expected to get an electric current just by putting a magnet near a wire, but it did not work out that way. The magnet and the wire had to move past each other.

It is like drying a wet handkerchief. If you hold the handkerchief still, it will hardly dry at all. However, if you blow air across it with an electric fan, or swish it through the air, it dries rapidly. It makes no difference whether the air moves and the handkerchief stays still or whether the air stays still and the handkerchief moves through it. It is necessary only to have one moving past the other. In Faraday's experiment all that was needed to produce the electric current was the motion of a magnet and a piece of wire past each other.

Faraday's keen mind found a way of picturing what

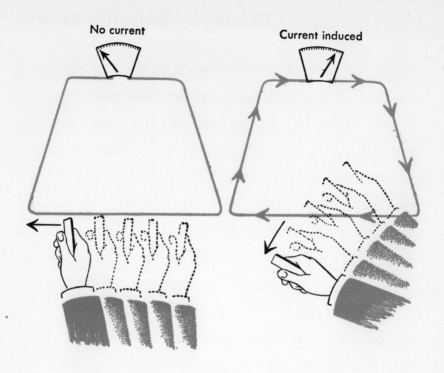

No current

Current induced

Current flows when lines of magnetic force cut across the wire.

happens when a current is set up by moving a magnet. You remember that a magnet has lines of force all around it (page 41). You can think of these lines as part of the magnet itself. If you move the magnet, the lines stay attached to it and move along with it. Faraday tried many ways of moving a magnet near a loop of wire. For example, if the magnet is moved along under a wire as in the first picture, nothing happens. But if it is moved crossways, as in the second picture, a current flows in the circuit when the magnet passes under the wire. The difference is that in the first trial, the lines of magnetic force just brushed along the sides of the wire; but in the second trial, the lines *cut across* it.

The same thing happens when a coil is used in place of a single wire. If the magnet just rests inside the coil, no lines of force cut across the windings; but as soon as the magnet is *moved*, they do cut across, and a current is set up. So Faraday saw that he could tell, in one sentence, what had to be done in any experiment where currents were set up by magnets. He said:

A current is produced whenever magnetic
lines of force cut across a wire that is part
of a complete circuit.

Any current that is produced by magnetism is now called an *induced* current.

A magnet moving in and out of a coil is really an *electric generator*, but it took more than thirty years to work out a practical one that could furnish current for electric lighting and other uses. The first real electric power station was started in New York City about seventy-five years ago. There were six generators turned by steam engines. The largest one was rated 125 horsepower, and it delivered current at 220 volts. This first

Huge generators at Hoover Dam send power 300 miles away.

generating station sold electric power to fifty-nine cus-
tomers and could give service for only a distance of one
mile in any direction. Now we have generators of over
100,000 horsepower that work at voltages as high as
20,000 and send their current hundreds of miles.

The gigantic Hoover Dam on the Colorado River
sends its power as far as Los Angeles, 300 miles away.
If you visit the dam you will be taken on a tour of the
power station. At the top of the dam, your party gets
into an elevator that whisks you silently down into the
very center of the huge concrete structure. In about a
minute, the car drops a distance greater than the height

of a 50-story building. Then you come out into a corridor. At the far end is one of the two power houses—a giant room over two city blocks long and as high as a big railroad station. Daylight streams in through the tall windows facing the river. Arranged along the side of the room are huge generators. Except for the faint whirring sound, nothing seems to be happening; yet the power of more than half a million wild horses is flowing out of these machines. This is enough power to take care of the household needs of 7 1/2 million people.

The simplest kind of generator is a loop of wire that can be turned on an axle. The loop is placed between

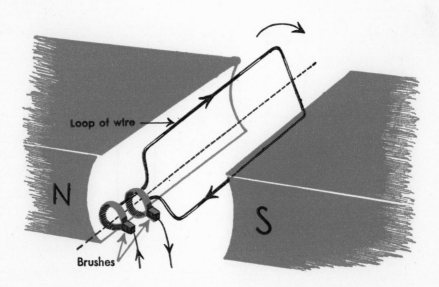

The turning loop cuts across the magnet's lines of force.

the poles of a magnet and each end of the loop is connected to a ring. The current is led away through brushes that touch the rings. If you turn the loop around and around, the wires forming the two long sides of the loop will cut across the lines of force of the magnet. This will induce a current in the loop, and this current will flow through any circuit connected to the brushes.

You might think that this current would be like the one from a battery, steady and always flowing in one direction. That is not what happens. The current from your simple generator flows first in one direction and

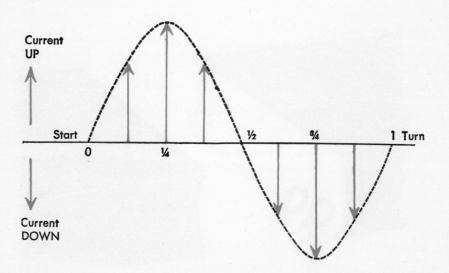

The current changes its direction as the loop turns around.

then in the other. It is called an *alternating* current, and electricians say "AC" for short.

If you follow what happens as the loop makes a complete turn, you find how this works out. After the loop has gotten halfway around, its sides begin to cut across the magnetic lines in the opposite direction; and this is what makes the induced current turn itself around after every half turn of the loop. The diagram shows how the current in the circuit changes as the loop turns clear around, starting from a straight up and down position. The length of each arrow stands for the strength of the current. Notice that the current is very small at first, getting bigger and bigger and then slackening off to nothing after half a turn. Now it starts getting larger in the opposite direction, finally dropping off to nothing at the end of a full turn. After that, everything repeats, one wave of current following another.

It may seem strange, but alternating current (AC) is better for most purposes than *direct* current (DC), which always flows in one direction. However, there are places where only DC can be used. For instance, in charging storage batteries, the charging current must be "pumped" into them always in one direction. The simple generator can be changed to give DC by replac-

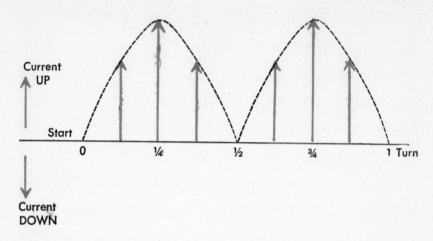

Current UP

Start

Current DOWN

| 0 | ¼ | ½ | ¾ | 1 Turn |

With a commutator, the current goes up after half a turn.

ing the two slip rings with a commutator just like the one on a motor (page 53). The commutator will then switch around the current that is sent out, so that instead of changing from upward to downward after half a turn, it will go upward again instead, as the next diagram shows.

This "commutated" current no longer goes back and forth, but it is far from *steady*. To make it steadier the engineers do the same thing as for the electric motor. In place of just a single loop, they wind many loops in slots spaced around the edge of the armature. Then, at times when some loops are furnishing little current, others are in a position to "fill in." The result is a very steady, direct current.

You can see that such a generator is built just like the motor that was described in the last chapter. Actually the same machine can be used either way. If you send current into it, the armature turns and you have a motor. If, instead, you turn the armature by hand or by using a steam engine or water wheel, it becomes a generator and you can get electric current from the brushes.

Why does it take such powerful engines or turbines to run the generators in a power station? The reason is that if we get electric power from a generator, we must put in at least the same amount of power in another form, such as steam or water power. All that any machine can do is to *change* one kind of power to another. It can never *make* power where there was none before.

There is a simple, hand-cranked generator in the emergency radio transmitter used in lifeboats. When the circuit is not connected, the crank turns very easily, but as soon as the switch is closed and electric power is being used, the crank becomes much harder to turn. The machine begins to drag and feels as if it were coated with molasses. The power needed to turn the crank comes from your muscles. The generator changes most of it into electric power.

CHAPTER 10

The Power Goes Far

At the very same time that Michael Faraday was working in London, Joseph Henry was experimenting with electromagnets in Albany, New York. In those days you could not simply go to the nearest store and buy insulated wire. It was not made. The people who wanted to experiment with electricity had to insulate their metal wires by giving them a coat of varnish.

Later some experimenters found exactly what they were looking for in an unexpected place. The ladies of that time wore fancy, tall hats that were stiffened with wire. This wire was covered with cotton, which is a good insulator, so here was a wire just made for electrical use. But Henry needed even better insulation in building his big electromagnets. The story is that he used strips of silk torn from his wife's old dresses.

Henry was the first person to wind several layers of insulated wire, one on top of the other, to make really strong electromagnets. One of his magnets was able to lift 3,500 pounds, which is about the weight of an automobile.

In one of his experiments, Henry wound a coil of copper wire on an iron bar and connected the ends of

Henry connected the coil to a meter clear across the room.

the coil to a meter many feet away. Then he laid the bar across the poles of his U-shaped electromagnet. When he sent current from a battery through the windings of the big magnet, the needle of the meter clear across the room jerked to one side, even though there was no actual electrical connection between the coil and the windings of the magnet. Then he cut the current off, and the needle jumped for an instant to the opposite side. This was just like what Faraday had found earlier when he jabbed a magnet in and out of a coil. In fact it *was* the same thing. It was just another way of getting an induced current. In the meantime, unknown to Henry, Faraday had done just about the same experiment.

Faraday had explained his earlier experiment with the coil and magnet by saying that currents must be induced whenever lines of magnetic force cut across wires. Moving the magnet in and out of the coil did this. But in the new experiment, nothing was moved. The magnet current was only switched on and off. Could it still be possible that lines of force cut across the wires? They really do, because when the current is started up in the windings of the electromagnet, we must think of the lines of force as springing up and

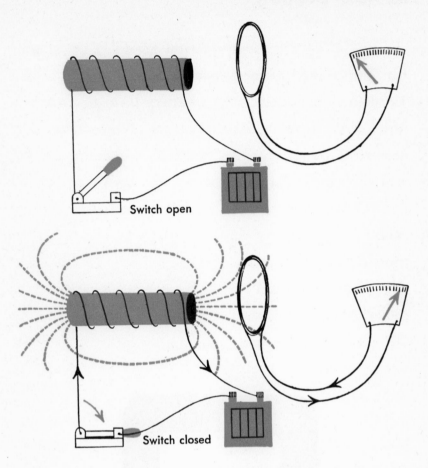

Switch open

Switch closed

When the current starts up, lines of force cut across the coil.

spreading out, as in the picture. But when this happens, the lines swish across the wires of the near-by coil, and this is what induces the current. In the same way, when the magnet current is turned off, the lines shrink down and cut across the coil again, giving an induced current in the opposite direction.

From these first experiments of Henry and Faraday, came the modern *transformer,* a device that makes it possible to send electric power over long distances. Transformers are an important part of telephone, radio and television systems too. In its simplest form, a transformer is made of two separate coils of wire wound on an iron ring, as in the picture. If current from a battery or a generator is sent through the first coil (called the *primary*), it magnetizes the ring. The lines of force stay inside the closed ring because it is easier for them to go through iron than through the surrounding air. But while these lines are building up, they shoot through

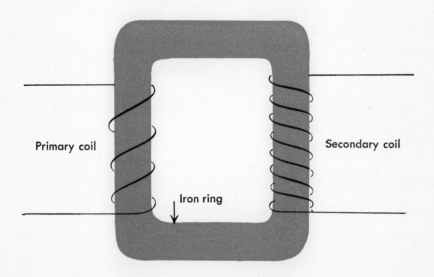

Primary coil   Secondary coil

Iron ring

A simple transformer has two coils of wire on an iron ring.

the other coil (called the *secondary*), and this induces a current in it as in Joseph Henry's experiment. When the current in the primary is cut off, there is a dash of current for just a moment in the secondary—then nothing more.

Henry found that he could change the voltage of the secondary current by changing the number of turns on the secondary coil. For example, if the secondary has twice as many turns as the primary, then the secondary voltage will be twice as great as the primary. The important thing the transformer does is to make it easy to *change the voltage of an electric current*.

There is a current in the secondary only at the instant the primary current is switched on or off. But if the current in the primary could be made to *change all the time*, then there would always be current in the secondary. This is exactly what happens with alternating current, which is just right for this purpose.

Out in the country you often see long electric power lines strung between tall steel towers. These lines may be a hundred miles long, sometimes even longer. If you come fairly near one of the towers, you may see a sign on it saying DANGER, 220,000 VOLTS. Why are such high voltages used? In sending a certain amount of power, you can use a weak current at high voltage or else a strong current at low voltage. On a power line the current should not be too large because this would require thick, heavy wires. Besides, the larger current would waste more power in the form of heat. So electrical engineers use *high voltage* and *low current* when power is to be sent over long distances.

Generators cannot work at too high a voltage because it is hard to insulate the different parts of the machine. But that is where transformers help out. For example, an AC generator may work at 10,000 volts. The current goes right into the primary coil of a huge transformer and is "stepped up" to 100,000 volts in the secondary coil and sent out over the lines. To boost the voltage ten times in this way, the secondary coil must have ten times as many turns as the primary.

When the power line reaches the edge of a town, it goes into a *substation*. A substation is usually an open yard with a steel framework overhead for carrying the lines. Underneath there are several transformers that look like big steel tanks. They are filled with oil that covers the windings completely. The oil helps insulate the windings and also keeps them cool. These transformers "step down" the voltage to about 20,000.

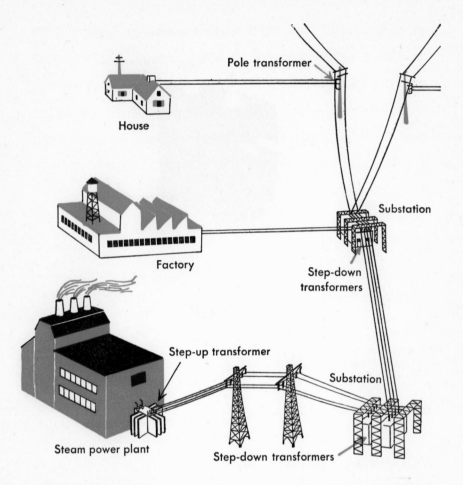

Pole transformer

House

Substation

Factory

Step-down
transformers

Step-up transformer

Substation

Steam power plant

Step-down transformers

High voltages are stepped down again for safe use in homes.

Outside a large steel mill there may be a smaller substation where transformers take off some current and
cut its voltage down to about 2,000 for running the
heavy machinery in the mill. Other substations farther
along the line lower the voltage to around 500 for the

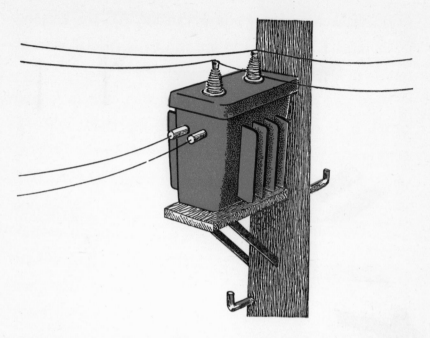

Transformers like this reduce power for safe use in homes.

use of factories. Finally, for safe use in your home, smaller transformers drop the power down to 115 volts. You can see these transformers mounted high on poles near your house.

In nearly all the power systems in the United States, the electrons in the wires are forced to flow back and forth 60 times a second. Engineers say that such an AC current has a *frequency of* 60 cycles. This is fast enough so that you never notice any flickering of the lamps in your home. The power companies keep the frequency so nearly steady that we now can use AC for keeping exact time. Electric clocks are run by a special kind of motor that stays right in step with the AC.

Now you understand why alternating current is used so much more than direct current, especially when it is to go to distant places. The use of AC makes it possible to change voltage by means of transformers. It is then possible to have high-voltage power lines, which use smaller, lighter wires and cut down heat losses too.

The transformer itself is really a marvelous device. It changes great amounts of electric power from one voltage to another with hardly any loss. It has no moving parts and makes no noise. Without it, our modern age of electric power would be impossible. But the usefulness of the transformer does not end there. In the following chapters you will find that many other important electrical devices depend on the transformer too.

CHAPTER 11

The Telephone

The man who made it possible to talk to someone thousands of miles away was always interested in the art of speaking. Even as a boy in Scotland, Alexander Graham Bell made a talking doll that could say, "Mama." Both his grandfather and his father had been teachers of speech, teaching deaf people to talk and training stammerers to speak properly. But when Bell made the first workable telephone, he was not thinking of speech at all. He was trying to improve the telegraph that Morse had invented nearly forty years earlier.

It was in Boston in the summer of 1875. The frontiers of the country were being pushed back rapidly, and settlers were moving into the West in large numbers. There was a great need for the telegraph in the new territories, and Bell was trying to find a way of sending several telegraph messages at the same time over a single line. He mounted a set of thin strips of steel above the pole of an electromagnet. From this he ran a line into another room and connected it to a second electromagnet. Above this second magnet he mounted another set of strips exactly like the first.

Bell was working in the second room when suddenly the instrument gave out a twanging sound. He rushed out to his assistant at the other end of the line, shouting excitedly, "What did you do then? Don't change anything! Let me see!"

The frightened helper stammered, "Why, sir, I merely snapped one of these strips, here, and it twanged back and forth for just a second or two." He hardly knew why his employer was so excited and was afraid he had done something wrong.

But Bell paid no attention. He was thinking hard. Now he understood what had happened. The fluttering strip had induced a current in the magnet coils, and it was this current that had gone over the line to make the strip in the other room move. Could he make the first strip move by using the sound of his voice instead of plucking it with his finger? Then, perhaps, the spoken words could be sent over the wire too. It was an exciting possibility. Alexander Bell thought far into the night, making sketches and figuring.

The next day he handed his assistant a drawing and asked him to make the first telephone. It looked like this:

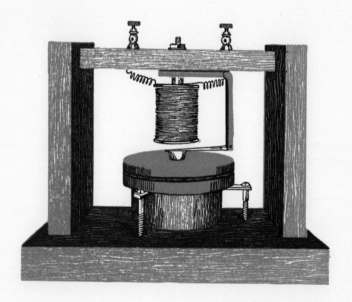

No one could recognize words over Bell's first telephone.

When someone spoke with his mouth close to the rubber membrane, faint tones could be heard coming from another such instrument at the other end of the line. It worked, but all that could be sent was the tone of the voice. Words could not be recognized. That took almost a year of experimenting. Soon the first outdoor telephone line was put up. It was two miles long.

To understand how the telephone works, you must first know certain facts about sound. If a stone is thrown into a quiet pond, ripples spread out in circles over the water. Sound travels through the air in the same way, in the form of waves, but sound waves are not exactly like the ones on water. Ripples on water have an up-and-down motion, while the air in a sound wave has a push-and-pull motion. Anything that can *vibrate* (shake back and forth very quickly) can send out sound waves. The strings of a piano can be made to vibrate, and so can the vocal cords in your throat. When sound waves hit your eardrum, it begins to flutter in step with the waves and you hear the sound.

In the simplest kind of telephone, the sound waves of your voice strike a thin iron disk and make it vibrate. The disk is mounted in front of an electromagnet, as in the diagram. Some of the lines of force of the magnet

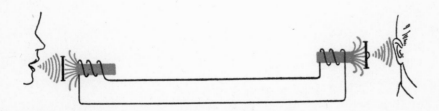

Sound waves from your voice send the current out over the wire.

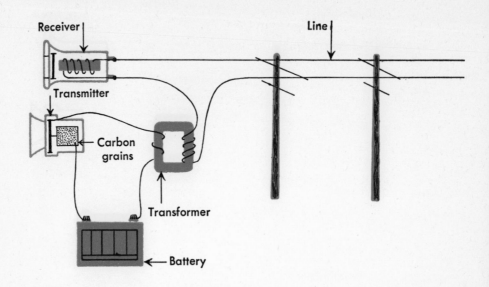

Sound waves produce a changing electrical current in the wire.

go through the iron disk. When it vibrates, these lines cut across the coil and set up an induced current in it. At the other end of the line, this current makes the strength of the magnet change in the same rhythm. As a result, the near-by iron disk is made to vibrate in step with the original sound waves. In doing this, it pushes on the air around it, sending out waves that are an exact copy of the ones from the speaker's voice. Notice that the sound waves themselves do not go out over the wire. Sound waves produce a changing electrical current in the wire, and this current produces another set of the *same* kind of waves at the far end of the line.

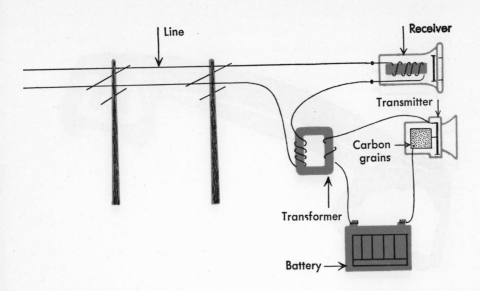

Line

Receiver

Transmitter

Carbon
grains

Transformer

Battery →

At the far end, the same kind of sound waves are given off.

Now for some improvements in this simplest telephone system. Batteries and transformers are used to give more powerful currents; and instead of a single electromagnet at each end of the line, there is a separate *transmitter* and *receiver*. The first transmitter was made by Thomas Edison. It was almost exactly like the ones used today. The main part is a little box filled with grains of carbon. One side of the box is connected to a thin metal disk. When sound waves make the disk vibrate, the carbon grains are pressed closer together and then loosened in turn. This controls the strength of the current that gets through from the battery. These

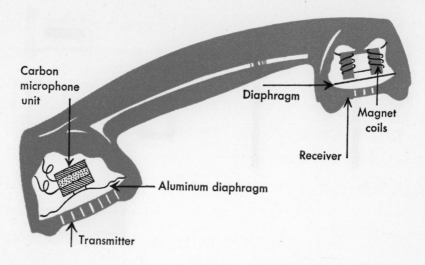

Carbon microphone unit

Diaphragm

Magnet coils

Receiver

Aluminum diaphragm

Transmitter

The modern hand set contains both transmitter and receiver.

changes in the current in the line are exactly like the changes in the sound waves of the speaker's voice.

The receiver at the other end of the line produces sound waves again, as already described. The system can carry messages in either direction. In a modern telephone the transmitter and receiver are both part of a single *hand set*, and the signaling bell and some other parts are in the base of the instrument.

Have you ever visited an automatic telephone exchange? Behind the switchboards themselves there is a confusing jumble of wires and rods and moving contacts that clatter and whir as they go about making connections. They seem to be moved by invisible hands. The whole scene is like something out of a science-fiction story.

Here is what happens when you dial a number on your telephone: When you turn the dial, it breaks in on the current in the lines a certain number of times as it goes back to its starting position. For example, if you dial the number 5, the current is cut off and put on again 5 times while the dial swings back. These short breaks in the current operate electromagnets that connect you with the number you are calling. One set of magnets lifts a contact piece to a certain row of contact points. Another set turns the contact piece to a particular point in the row. The combination of numbers that you dial is what picks out the exact circuit of the telephone you want to call.

Besides this, the machines must produce the dial tone that tells you the line is ready to take your call; and they must ring the bell at the other end of the line. If the line is in use, they must put on the busy signal. And, after the call is finished, they must make a record of it so that the company can figure its cost. Finally, there is a machine that automatically checks the selector devices one after another. If it finds anything wrong, it rings a bell and lights a lamp that shows where the faulty part is located.

On long-distance lines, the machinery is even more complicated. If the connection cannot be made at once, the number is "stored up" while the machine automatically checks hundreds of circuits until it finds one that is free. The system is like a huge electrical brain that works a hundred times faster than the human brain.

Modern telephone systems work a little differently from the simple arrangement shown on page 81. They use very rapid electrical vibrations that are something like radio waves, except that they move along wires instead of through space. The cross-country lines are carried in underground cables. Each cable is only about as thick as your arm, but it can carry hundreds of telephone conversations as well as several television programs and teletype messages all at the same time.

Bell's rough invention has developed into the modern telephone within the short space of a single lifetime. Today there are more than 75 million telephones in use all over the world. With the help of radio hookups for getting across the oceans, any two of these telephones can be connected almost immediately.

There is now an undersea telephone cable in service between North America and Europe. The cable makes it possible to carry on clear conversations under all kinds of weather conditions, untroubled by static or fading. Of all modern electrical wonders, the telephone is certainly one of the greatest.

CHAPTER 12

Waves
Around the World

The gale whipped and howled around the old watch-tower on the hill above the harbor. Far below lay the little town of St. Johns, Newfoundland. Its little wooden houses, clustered close to the water front, seemed to snuggle together to protect themselves from the storm.

Up on the hill, a lone man was trying to get a box kite into the air. It dipped and swayed but finally stayed up, tugging powerfully on its string. From the kite, a wire looped down and led through a window into a room on the upper floor of the tower. Here a number of men were grouped around a table covered with electrical equipment. In the center of the group sat a serious young man, staring out into space. From time to time he sipped from a cup of hot cocoa or glanced nervously at the clock on the wall. Clamped over his ears was a pair of head telephones connected to one of the instruments in front of him. He was the Italian experimenter Guglielmo Marconi. It was shortly after noon of December 12, 1901.

When would the signal come? Marconi had been working toward this day for many years. Even as a boy, he had managed to put together some homemade equipment that sent a signal across a room without any connecting wires. Then he was able to make the signals more powerful and send them a distance of a mile, then twelve miles. Just two years before he waited in that cold tower above St. Johns harbor, his "wireless" signals were used for the first time to bring help to shipwrecked sailors. Now he was hoping to receive a signal from a station all the way across the Atlantic in England.

Everything had been arranged in advance. The English station was to send out the Morse code signal for the letter "S," three short dots. Every day, beginning at noon, it was to send this signal over and over again. Back in Europe the experts had told Marconi that the

Nervously, Marconi waited for the signal to come from England.

signals would never follow the curve of the earth but would spread out in space and miss the receiver altogether.

It was now about 12:30. Marconi nibbled on a piece of bread. He was about to take off the receivers and give up for that day. Just at that moment, above the howling of the wind and the crackling of static in the earphones, he heard three faint clicks! They came again and again. The men around him saw by his face that something was happening. They pressed closer.

Marconi ripped off the headphones and handed them to an assistant. "Do you hear anything?" he asked in a trembling voice.

"I certainly do—I'm sure of it!" was the excited reply. The headset was quickly handed around from one man to another. There was no doubt about it. A wireless signal had come around the curve of the world to carry its message nearly two thousand miles.

Marconi never doubted that he would succeed in making wireless a practical way of sending messages over long distances. Now he had all the proof he needed. Within a few years he started a regular news service between England and the United States and later organized a company for sending business messages. In 1912, after the sinking steamship *Titanic* was able to send out an SOS for help, Marconi began to receive many honors for his great work.

Most inventions do not develop through the work of just one person. So it was with wireless. Marconi proved that wireless was a practical way of sending messages, but the scientific discovery that made this possible was actually known ten years before Marconi was born.

In order to see how this worked out, think again of water instead of electricity. Imagine a U-shaped tube, like the one in the picture. At the bottom, there is a valve that can be opened and closed. The water can flow from one part of the U to the other only when the valve is open.

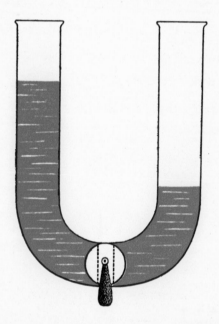

To start with, suppose you shut the valve and pour water into both sides of the U-tube. Put more water in

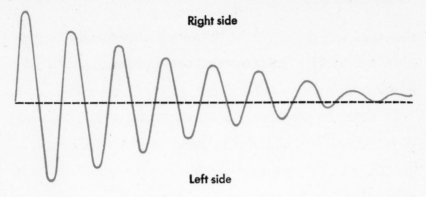

Right side

Left side

the left-hand tube than in the right. Now quickly open the valve. The water rushes from left to right, but it does not stop the first time it reaches the same level in the two tubes. Instead it piles up higher on the right for a moment, then surges back until it is again high on the left, but not quite so high as it was at first. This surging back and forth keeps up until the swings, getting weaker all the time, finally die out.

Here is an electrician's diagram of a circuit that does

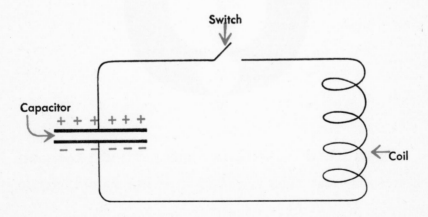

Switch

Capacitor

+ + + + + +

− − − − −

←**Coil**

exactly the same thing. The *capacitor* is a device that is very useful in all sorts of electric circuits, such as telephones, radios, and so on. The simplest capacitor is a pair of large metal sheets separated by a thin layer of insulating material. Putting a charge on one plate is just like putting more water in one side of the U-tube. As soon as the switch is closed, the charge starts to rush back and forth through the coil, piling up first on one plate of the capacitor, then on the other, until the current finally dies out.

In the U-tube, the water surfaces, surging up and down, beat on the surrounding air and send out sound waves. Of course in this case the waves follow each other so slowly that the sound cannot be heard, but the waves are there just the same.

Does the electric circuit send out some sort of wave too? An English scientist named Maxwell figured out that this would happen, and that the waves would be *electrical waves* that could move even through empty space. In fact, they would be wireless waves! He found that electrical waves and light waves are of the same kind, and that all such waves move through space with the same tremendous speed of 186,000 miles a second. The only real difference between wireless waves and light waves is the distance between the humps. For the light waves that your eye can see, this distance is only about a hundred-thousandth of an inch. It is around a quarter of a mile for wireless waves, or what we now call *radio waves*.

Maxwell had worked all this out on paper, but it took over twenty years before anyone found a way to produce electrical waves and prove that they acted like light waves. Heinrich Hertz, a German experimenter, was the first one to do this. He found that the waves could be reflected from a metal screen in just the same way that light is reflected from a mirror. These waves could be gathered into a beam and sent across space. But in one way they seemed different from the kind of waves that we can see. Electrical waves pass right through a solid material, as long as it is not made of metal or some other conductor.

Hertz was able to pick up his waves only a few feet away. Then Marconi found that he could send them part way around the earth by using a circuit like the one shown in the picture. When the key is pressed down, current flows in the windings of the transformer and a charge starts to build up on the capacitor. The potential difference across the plates gets larger and

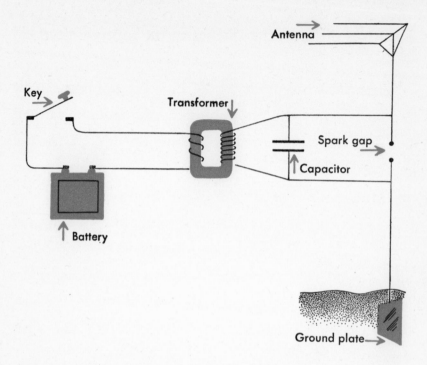

Key

Transformer

Antenna

Spark gap

Capacitor

Battery

Ground plate

This wireless circuit can send messages around the earth.

larger until, all at once, there is a spark across the gap. All this takes place in about a thousandth of a second.

When the spark flashes over, the charge surges back and forth in the circuit just as the water swished from one side to the other in the tube. Electrons are much lighter than water, so they swing back and forth much faster. They may vibrate with a frequency of a million or more each second. Part of the power of these surges is thrown off from the antenna in the form of electrical waves.

Since the current that goes into the sending circuit is controlled by the telegraph key, the operator can tap out dots and dashes to send his message in code. At the receiving station a similar circuit picks up the waves and gives a signal in a telephone or loud speaker.

So here we have wireless, sending news across the world with the speed of light, saving lives at sea, doing all kinds of work. But before engineers could make the jump from wireless to radio as we now know it, something else was needed. The next chapter tells what that is.

CHAPTER 13

Electron Tubes

Have you ever noticed that the tubes in a modern radio look very much like small electric light bulbs? This did not happen just by chance. The light bulb really is a sort of grandfather to the radio tube.

It all started about seventy-five years ago. Thomas Edison was making some further experiments with the electric light, which he had invented a short time before. He sealed a metal rod into the side of a light bulb and connected it to one post of a battery. The other post he connected to a switch and a meter and then to one side of the lamp filament. He found that a current would flow when the rod was joined to the *plus* terminal of the battery, but not when connected to the minus. This meant that a current would somehow go

Edison found that current flowed from the filament to the rod.

across the empty space between the filament and the rod, but only in one direction.

Edison made a note of this discovery, but he did nothing more about it. And so he missed inventing one of the most important devices ever made. The radio tube, which is based on this "Edison effect," proved to be just as valuable an invention as the electric light. Nobody can blame Edison for not following up this curious effect. At that time it did not seem to have any practical use. Later, after the electron had been discovered, scientists could explain what went on and could see ways of putting this discovery to work.

The great crowds of free electrons inside a metal are continually jumping around, hitting each other all the time. If the metal is heated, the jumping gets wilder and wilder; and some of the electrons are knocked clear out of the metal. It is very much like steam coming from a pot of boiling water. When the wire is made as hot as the filament in a lamp (more than 4,000 degrees), about 5 billion billion electrons jump out every second. This is a good and easy way of getting electrons all by themselves.

In an ordinary electric bulb, the electrons that come off form a cloud around the filament. As more and more electrons come away, the cloud gets thicker. Soon there are just as many electrons wandering back to the filament as there are coming out; and a sort of balance is reached. In Edison's tube the electrons in the cloud were pulled over to the rod when it was charged plus. They rushed across the space, entered the rod and went clear around the circuit. This was the current that Edison noticed. But when the rod was connected to the minus terminal of the battery, the minus charge pushed back the electron cloud and stopped the current in the circuit. The electrons could go across from the hot

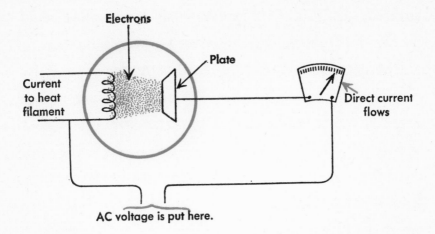

The electrons can go only from the hot filament to the plate.

filament to the rod, but not the other way. This special lamp was like a valve that lets water flow one way only, or like a turnstile which allows people to pass through a gate in only one direction.

Scientists in England and Germany quickly discov-

ered uses for this new kind of lamp, or vacuum tube. They found it could change AC to DC. One side of the AC wave current is held back, leaving only a set of DC peaks on the other side. By hooking up other tubes, coils and capacitors, a very steady DC current can be gotten. The tube was also found very useful in a wireless receiver.

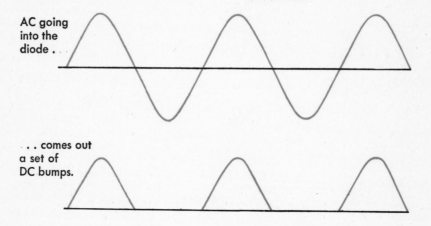

AC going into the diode .

. . . comes out a set of DC bumps.

The diode can change AC to DC.

The collecting rod was later replaced by a metal plate to gather the electrons more easily. Instead of placing the plate on the opposite side of the tube, it was bent around the filament. The tube was beginning to look more and more like the radio tubes of today. It was finally called a *diode*.

The biggest improvement of all was made by a young American scientist and inventor, Lee De Forest. His idea was really very simple. It was so simple that, for a long time, nobody would believe it could work. But it did work, and it gave us the modern telephone, radio, television and many other wonders of electronics.

De Forest thought of putting a wire screen in the tube, placing it between the filament and the plate. He would use this screen (now called the *grid*) to control the electrons coming from the filament. With the grid added, the tube is called a *triode*. The picture shows how the parts of a triode are arranged. The grid is curved around the filament, and the plate is then curved around the grid. Suppose the plate is kept plus-charged while nothing is done to the grid. Then the electrons that come out of the hot filament will be pulled across to the plate. In doing so they pass right through the holes in the grid.

Now give the grid a small minus charge. Being very close to the filament, it will hold back the swarm of electrons and so cut down the current to the plate. The important thing is that a *very small* change in the voltage of the grid can make a *large* change in the current across the tube. It is like batting a ball. A small move-

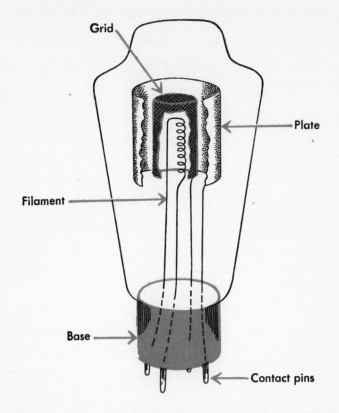

Grid

Plate

Filament

Base

Contact pins

With a grid added, the tube is called a triode.

ment of your wrists makes the end of the bat swing in a big circle. The bat increases the action of the wrists; the tube *amplifies* the voltage that is put onto the grid.

A single triode usually steps up changes in voltage until they are five to twenty times what they were. By using several triodes, one after another, the original voltage may be amplified billions of times. The plate of the first tube is connected to the grid of the second one, and the plate of the second tube is connected to the grid of the next, and so on. Suppose the voltage changes are amplified ten times by each triode. Then, after going through only six stages, the voltage changes would be amplified $10 \times 10 \times 10 \times 10 \times 10 \times 10$, or one million times!

Amplifiers of this kind are important parts of radio circuits. They are also used in many scientific experiments where tiny electrical currents have to be picked up and measured. Doctors find that very weak ripples of electrical voltage are produced in the living body. The action of your heart does this, for example. These voltages can be taken to an amplifier through wires held in contact with the skin. After they are magnified in this way, the ripples can be studied to find out the condition of your heart.

CHAPTER 14

Radio

The invention of vacuum tubes, especially the triode, opened up the possibility of many new developments. One of the most important of these was radio. In the broadcasting station there are the transmitting circuits that put the programs "on the air." Here the triode is in command. It keeps the current swinging back and forth in the circuits.

Suppose the coils and capacitors in these circuits are adjusted so that the current makes one million vibrations each second. The current is amplified and carried to the antenna, which then sends out radio waves of the same frequency. Radio engineers would say that this station was sending out waves at a frequency of 1,000 *kilocycles*. One *kilocycle* means one *thousand cycles*, or a thousand waves each second, so 1,000 kilocycles would be our million-a-second wave from this broadcasting station. Here is how you can picture such a wave:

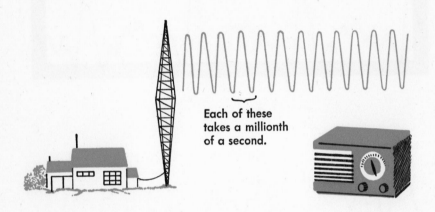

Each of these takes a millionth of a second.

Now what happens when your radio receiving set picks up this *carrier wave?* The answer is—"Nothing!" The reason is that the loud-speaker of your receiving set cannot be made to vibrate anywhere near as fast as a million times a second. It is too heavy and slow-moving, and so would not give out any sound at all.

In order for you to be able to hear speech or music on your radio, the carrier waves from the broadcasting station must first be "worked on" by the sound waves that are being broadcast. Every sound wave, whether it is from the voice or from a musical instrument, has its own special *shape*. For instance, this is a diagram of how the air is pushed back and forth when you sing "ah:"

And these are sound waves from a note played on a clarinet:

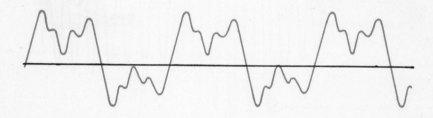

Now suppose that at a certain moment this sound wave is hitting the microphone in the broadcasting station:

The microphone changes the sound wiggles into voltage wiggles *of the same shape*, and these voltages are fed into the circuits. Here they modulate the carrier waves, holding down their vibrations and making them take the exact shape of the original sound wave. The picture shows what happens. The individual waves are still the 1,000-kilocycle ones, but their height changes in step with the sound waves that are being broadcast.

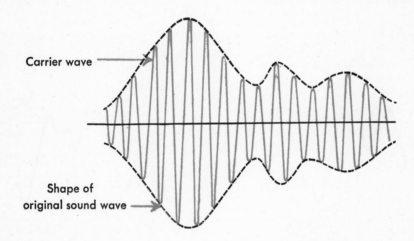

Carrier wave

Shape of
original sound wave

A carrier wave takes the shape of the original sound wave.

At the receiving end the waves are picked up by the antenna or perhaps just by a coil in the set itself. The carrier waves induce a current of the same frequency in the first circuit of your set. But they can do this only if your set is *tuned* to the station you want to listen to.

Think of a child's swing. Once started, it swings

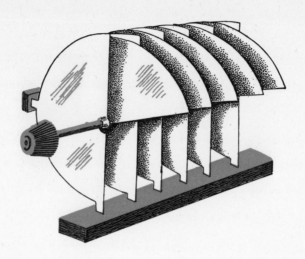

To change stations on your radio, you use a capacitor.

back and forth a certain number of times a minute. If you want to make the swing go high, you can do it by pushing it in time with its natural frequency. If you were to push it at a different rate, you would not be able to build up its motion. Some of the pushes would cancel out the effect of some others because they would come at the wrong times.

The same thing is true of the circuit in the radio set. You turn the tuning knob until the current in the circuit can swing back and forth with the same frequency as the carrier wave of the station you want to pick up. Look into the back of your set while turning the knob. You will see that the knob turns a set of movable metal plates. They are part of a capacitor. Moving these plates in or out changes the natural frequency of current in the circuit, just as changing the length of the ropes would change the frequency of the swing.

Each broadcasting station in your part of the country must keep its carrier wave at a certain frequency at all times. The Federal Communications Commission makes sure that each station keeps at the exact frequency it has been given. Your radio dial is marked with numbers that run from 55 to 160. This means you can tune in on frequencies from 550 to 1600 kilocycles, one after another. For instance, when your set is tuned to receive a station broadcasting at 710 kilocycles, it will pick up waves of this frequency only, and no others will affect it.

Now that the proper carrier wave has been picked up in the first circuit, the sound message riding on it must be unscrambled. A triode does this in a neat way. It squeezes down one side of the set of modulated carrier waves until they look like this:

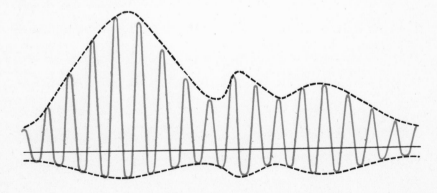

These new waves are amplified by a string of other triodes and then sent to the coil of a loud-speaker. Now that the current waves are one-sided, they are able to move the coil of the loud-speaker back and forth to make the speaker give out a copy of the original sound waves. They can do this because the other side of the waves is no longer there to cancel things out.

There are many ways of designing the circuits for radio broadcasting and receiving, but they all work according to the same scientific rules. Always the original sound waves are turned into electric current changes whose pattern is put onto the carrier waves. The carrier waves go out and are picked up by the receiving circuit, where they are again turned into a changing electric current. This pattern is "picked off" and changed into sound waves once more by the loud-speaker.

Changing the height of the carrier waves is called *amplitude modulation* (AM). In the past few years, another way of modulating the carrier waves has been coming into use. It is called *frequency modulation* (FM). Instead of changing the height of the carrier waves, their frequency is changed to match the sound. The sound waves squeeze the carrier waves together at some places and stretch them out at others. The advantage is that electrical disturbances caused by lightning and by sparks from electrical machines cannot get through when FM is used, and so the sound received is clear and sharp.

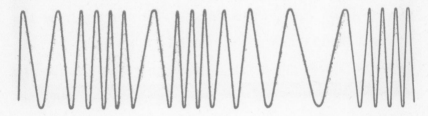

In FM, the frequency of the waves is changed, not the height.

CHAPTER 15

Electrons and Light

The triode can do many wonderful things all by it-self, but it can work even greater magic when it is teamed up with another kind of vacuum tube called a *photocell* ("photo" is from the Greek word for light). This busy little device gives us television and puts the sound track onto motion-picture films. It automatically opens doors, sorts out food products and acts as a burglar alarm. It detects smoke, helps us to take better pictures and does a great variety of other things. In whatever way you use it, a photocell does just one thing. It changes a beam of light into a current of electricity.

The *photoelectric effect* (which is the name for what goes on in a photocell) was discovered by Hertz when

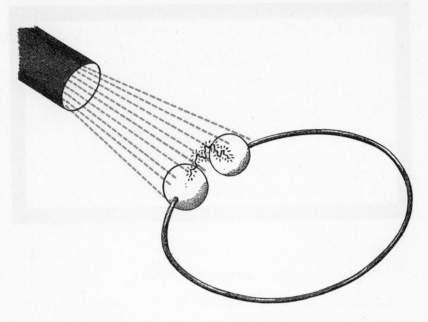

The spark jumps more readily when light shines on the metal.

he was experimenting with electric waves (see page 94). To check on the arrival of the waves, he let them form a tiny spark across a gap in the receiving circuit. Sometimes the spark was weak, even when the circuit was carefully tuned to the incoming waves. Hertz happened to shine a light on the metal balls that formed the spark gap. He found that this made the spark jump across much more easily. But he was more interested in wireless waves at that time, and so he did nothing further about the photoelectric effect.

Other experimenters found that a clean piece of metal would get a small plus charge of electricity when light was allowed to shine on it. A few years later, after the discovery of the electron, scientists began to understand what went on. *Under certain conditions, light can shake electrons out of a metal.* It was these electrons that strengthened the spark in Hertz's wireless circuit. And it was these electrons, jumping out of an insulated piece of metal, that left the metal with a plus charge.

Albert Einstein was able to work out an exact mathematical rule for the photoelectric effect. Before long, scientists were testing Einstein's rule in their laboratories. They checked the fact that the electron stream from a metal becomes stronger as the light is made brighter. If the brightness is doubled, the current of electrons will double. And they found that the electrons start coming out as soon as the light hits the metal. The instant the light is shut off, the electron stream stops too. This means that the photoelectric current can be made to follow very fast changes in the strength of a beam of light. That is what makes the effect so useful.

The picture shows a photocell. Part of the inside of the glass bulb is coated with a special metal, such as potassium. Near the center of the tube there is a loop

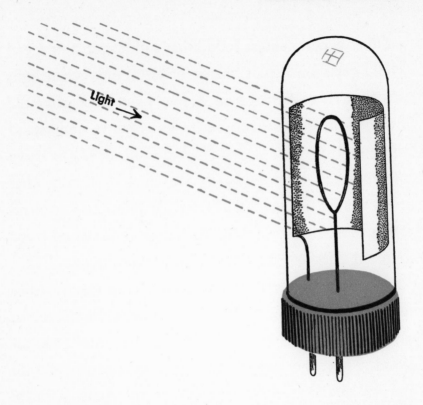

Light →

When light shines on the coating, electrons are thrown off.

of metal connected to the outside by a wire. Another wire leads out from the potassium coating. These wires are joined to a battery and a sensitive ammeter, the plus terminal of the battery being connected to the loop.

Now, when light is allowed to shine on the coating, electrons are thrown off. The air has been pumped out of the tube so that the electrons can go straight across to the loop. Then they keep going around the circuit, and the meter registers a current as long as the light shines on the cell.

The electron current in a photocell is usually only a few millionths of an ampere. It is too weak to do more than move the pointer of a delicate meter. But this is where the photocell is helped out by its cousin, the triode. By using an amplifier, the tiny photoelectric current can be built up until it is strong enough to work an electromagnet. Then the electromagnet can close a switch to turn on a current of any amount that is needed.

One of the most remarkable uses of the photocell is to produce the sound track for motion pictures. When the film is photographed in the studio, the sound is

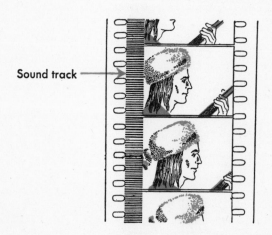

Sound track

Sound is recorded on the film alongside the pictures.

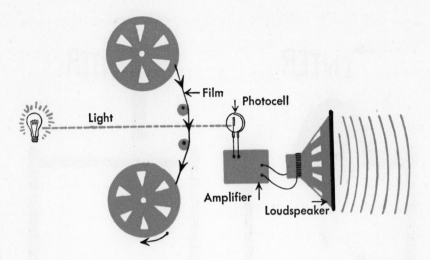

The sound track controls the amount of light to the photocell.

recorded on the film alongside the pictures. To do this, a microphone picks up the sound waves and changes them into an electric current. By means of an amplifier and an electromagnet, this current is made to open and close a narrow slit. A light shines through the slit onto the moving film. As the sound waves work the slit, the sound track is formed on the film. After it is developed, the sound track looks like a set of light and dark stripes.

When the film is being shown in a theater, a special lamp mounted in the projector sends light through the sound track to a photocell. The sound track controls the amount of light that reaches the photocell. These changes of the light make the same kind of changes in

Lamp

Photocell

When the light beam is blocked, a photocell opens the door.

the current in the cell. All that is needed is to amplify the current and pass it to a loud-speaker, and you hear the proper sound along with the pictures on the screen.

For many other uses, the photocell hookup can be much simpler. For instance, the cell can be arranged to open a door automatically. When a person crosses the beam of light, this stops the current in the cell, a switch contact drops down and starts an electric motor that swings the door open. After a few seconds a special switch cuts off the motor current, and a spring slowly closes the door again.

A similar arrangement can be used to turn on the water in a drinking fountain. As you bend over to drink, you cut across a beam of light and the photocell turns on the water. Or a beam of light along the front of a machine such as a punch press can be used to protect the operator from injury. If he should happen to get his hand in the way of the moving parts, a photocell will stop the machine at once.

A photoelectric burglar alarm can be set up in much the same way. Whenever the light beam is broken, the alarm goes off. By using the proper kind of metal coating on the cell, the system can be worked with a beam of invisible light ("black light") so that nobody even knows the alarm setup is there.

There seems to be no limit to the number of inventions that make use of photocells. A beam of light can be used to count things as they go by on a moving belt. Each time one article, such as a tin can, goes past, it breaks the beam and makes a photocell turn a counting device.

A photoelectric arrangement can even take the place of an inspector in a factory. The product to be inspected may be oranges, for example, passing along on a moving belt. This time the light beam is arranged so that it is reflected from the fruit and then goes to the photocell. A green orange that happens to be in the pack will reflect a different amount of light than a ripe one. The change in current from the cell works an electromagnet that pushes the bad piece of fruit off the belt.

There are other kinds of photocells besides the vacuum tube type. One, called a *barrier-layer* cell, generates its own current and needs no battery. It uses a thin layer of copper oxide on a copper disk. When light hits the copper oxide, it makes electrons go over to the copper disk. These electrons flow around a complete circuit through a sensitive meter that tells how strong a light is falling on the cell. The exposure meters used by photographers usually have barrier-layer photocells in them. By measuring the strength of the light, the photographer knows how to set his camera to get a properly exposed picture.

Another important kind of photocell makes use of *semi-conductors*. Semi-conductors are materials that have an electrical resistance just about halfway between metals like copper and insulators like glass. Semi-conductors can do many interesting things. Some kinds can set electrons free when light strikes them, and these serve as a new kind of photocell. Another sort does just the

A sun battery powers this telephone line.

opposite thing. It gives off light when electrons strike it. This kind of semi-conductor is used to coat the end of the picture tube in your television set.

Semi-conductors are used in a device called the *transistor*, which is a tiny bit of semi-conducting material with wires joined to it. This "mighty midget" of electronics seems to be taking over most of the jobs that vacuum tubes used to do.

The semi-conductors used in transistors are unusual

A transistor (shown at the left) is smaller than a stamp.

materials that have either too many or too few electrons in them. If there are too many, the extra ones can move through the material as they would through a vacuum. If there are too few electrons, the empty spaces move along through the semi-conductor when the remaining electrons shift their places. When these "holes" move, it is just as if actual plus charges were being carried along. The movement of the electrons or of the holes can be controlled by sending in tiny voltages, just as the current in a triode can be regulated by small voltages put on the grid.

Besides being much smaller in size, transistors have great advantages over vacuum tubes. Transistors are always ready for work. There is no filament that needs time to warm up before electrons boil off. There is no vacuum to go bad, and nothing to burn out. Transistors last for many years. And most important of all, they work much more efficiently than vacuum tubes.

The small size of the transistor and the fact that it needs so little power are great advantages. Electrical engineers can now build a hearing aid no bigger than a pack of cigarettes and a portable two-way radio small enough to be carried in your pocket. Some of the new electronic calculating machines ("electric brains") use nearly 20,000 vacuum tubes. You can imagine how much heat they give off. Replacing the tubes with transistors solves the heat problem and allows the whole machine to be put in a much smaller space.

A two-way transistor FM radio set fits into a soldier's helmet.

All About Electricity

Almost every day new uses are being discovered for transistors. In the years to come, these busy gadgets will probably make the vacuum tube look as old-fashioned as the oil lamp!

CHAPTER 16

Television

There is much more to television than just adding a picture to radio. It must be a moving picture, and the sound must be "in step" with it. And now people prefer to have the picture in natural color. All this makes television a complicated matter. Coils and capacitors, vacuum tubes and photocells are used in television sets; but some new and even more tricky devices than any of these are also needed.

The beginnings of television go back less than thirty years. Today there are nearly 45 million sets in the world, most of them in the United States. Television is one of our fastest growing industries.

In television the picture you see on your set at any

instant is not really there all at once, like a lantern slide flashed on a screen. Each picture must first be "taken apart" at the broadcasting station and sent to the distant receiver by electric waves. Then the parts must be "put together" again in your set to form the original picture. All this must take place in less than the wink of an eye. Many pictures must be sent out each second so that your eye sees a steady movement, just as in watching motion pictures.

At this point the electron comes along to help out. Electrons, being light in weight, can be sent scurrying back and forth across the picture, scanning every bit of it as they go. In your receiving set another group of electrons can be made to brush across every part of the screen, filling in the picture for you to see.

At the broadcasting studio the camera lens forms a small light picture of the scene, just as every camera lens does. Instead of falling on a photographic film, the light picture hits a square of photoelectric material in the *pickup tube*, and electrons are set free. At the bright spots in the picture, more electrons come off. At the dark places, fewer break away. The electrons shoot straight across a vacuum to the target, which is not much bigger than a postage stamp. Wherever these elec-

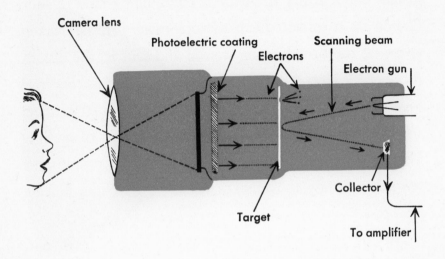

The pickup tube changes the picture into electrical signals.

trons hit the target, they knock other electrons out and leave a plus charge at that spot.

Now still other electrons come into the story. A steady stream of electrons from the *electron gun* at the far right side of the tube is shot at the target and bounces back again to the collector. But while this electron beam is at the turn-around point, it is "tickled" by the charges that happen to be at that place on the target.

The beam is made to sweep across the target, line after line, over and over again. As a result the beam is changed (modulated) as it "reads" all the places on the

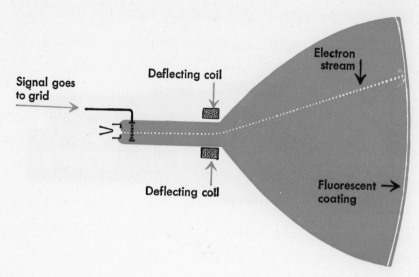

Picture signals control the strength of the electron beam.

picture, and the current coming from the collector changes to match.

This current is amplified and goes into the antenna where it controls the electric waves on which the picture is being broadcast. The picture message has been handed on from one set of electrons to another in a sort of relay race.

At the receiving end the waves induce tiny voltages in the antenna on top of your house. These voltages are amplified and put on the control grid of your picture tube. The inside of the front of the tube is coated with a *fluorescent* material that glows when electrons hit it. As the picture signals come in to the grid, they change the strength of the electron beam, making the spot where it hits the screen brighter or fainter.

This spot must not stand still. It must sweep across the end of the tube to "paint" the picture in light, just as the electron beam in the pickup tube had to sweep across the target. And the two beams, one at the broadcasting station and the other in your set, must be kept right in step with each other by a special regulating signal.

Electron beam

An electron beam sweeps across the end of the tube, line by line.

Two pairs of coils make the electron beam sweep the end of the picture tube. One pair moves the beam across the end of the tube from left to right. It then snaps the beam back to the left again as the other pair moves the beam down a short distance, ready to trace the next line. The electron beam moves the way your eyes do when you read a book.

The beam sweeps across the tube in 525 lines to form each picture. To get the best picture, it sweeps over *every other* line from top to bottom, then goes back and fills in the lines between. All this must be done fast enough to give the appearance of a steady picture. To make sure of this, the scenes are traced at the rate of thirty a second. This means that the spot at the tip of the electron beam whizzes along the screen of your home receiver at a tremendous speed. While you watch an hour and a half show, the little spot goes the distance around the earth!

The electrical waves that carry television programs have much higher frequencies than radio waves. Radio wave frequencies are measured in kilocycles (page 106), but television frequencies are measured in *megacycles*. A megacycle is a million cycles (or waves) each second. For the stations now in service, the frequencies go up to nearly 1,000 megacycles. Each television channel to which you tune your set has a certain frequency. The sound part of the program comes in on a separate FM wave.

Color television equipment is even more complicated than the usual black-and-white kind. You might think that a separate signal would be needed for every color you wanted to have in the picture. Luckily it is not quite as bad as that. Scientists know that you can get a very good copy of all the colors simply by mixing three *primary* colors in different amounts. That is how color is shown in films and in much color printing. The primary colors used are certain shades of red, green and blue. This means that three sets of signals must be transmitted for color television, one for each primary color.

The camera at the broadcasting station has three pickup tubes, each with a piece of colored glass in front of it. If, for instance, there is an American flag in the scene, the red stripes will send light through the red glass to the pickup tube behind it. However, no light from these stripes will get through the green or blue glasses. The blue field of the flag will register only on the second tube, after getting through the blue glass. The white stars and white stripes will send some light through each of the three glasses, just the right amounts to give a mixture that looks white. Each pickup tube puts out its own set of voltage changes, which are amplified in the usual way. Then they are used, one after the other, to shape the carrier waves.

In color television the fluorescent coating on the end of the picture tube is no longer of one kind. Instead it must be made up of tiny dots of the material arranged in groups of three. One dot glows red when the elec-

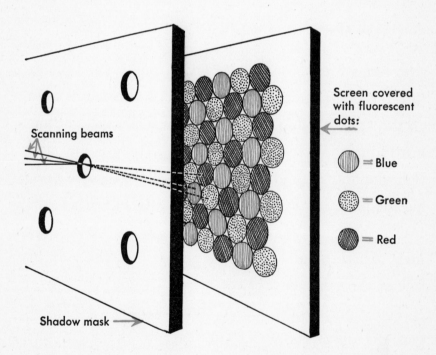

Holes in the shadow mask direct the beams to the proper spots.

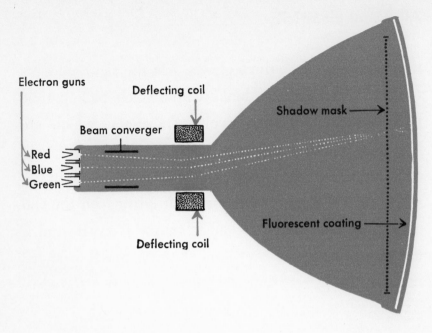

Electron guns

Deflecting coil

Beam converger

Shadow mask ——→

Red
Blue
Green

Deflecting coil

Fluorescent coating ——→

Each electron gun gets the signal for one color.

tron beam hits it, one glows green, one blue. Just before the electron beam hits the end of the tube it must go through a shadow mask. This is a metal plate having many, many very small holes in it. There is one hole right opposite each group of dots. You can see that making the plate and lining it up are no easy jobs when you realize that there are nearly 2,000 holes to every square inch. Three separate electron guns are placed side by side at the other end of the tube.

You can guess the rest of the description. Each gun gets the signal for one color. Because the three guns are in slightly different places, each one "sees" only one kind of dot through the holes in the plate. When a "blue" signal comes along, it goes to the "blue" gun. This shoots out a burst of electrons that come through the holes in the direction of the blue dots on the screen. The same for the other two primary colors and any mixtures of these colors. The result is a picture in sparkling, true color.

That is how modern science has put the electron to work to bring us the natural sights and sounds of distant events while they are happening. It is a good example of how electricity has made our lives safer, more comfortable and more interesting.

Index

Index

Carbon, as conductor, 26
Carbon atom, 15
Carrier waves, 107, 108, 109, 111, 112
Cells, of battery, 27, 31
Channel, television, 133
Charge, 6, 24, 42
  minus, 10, 11, 14, 15, 17, 18, 22
  neutralized by earth, 20
  plus, 10, 11, 14, 15, 17, 18, 22, 23
  spread of, 18
Circuit, definition of, 31
Clock, electric, 56, 77
Coils, in transformer, 72, 73, 74
Collector, in television, 129, 130
Color television, 133-36
Colors, primary, 133
Commutator, and armature, 53, 54, 55
  and DC current, 66
Compass, 35, 38, 39, 43, 44
Conductors, definition of, 18
Copper, in barrier-layer photocell, 122
  in battery, 26, 27
  as conductor, 19, 26
Cotton, as insulator, 68
Current, alternating, 64-65, 76, 102
  direct, 65, 66, 102
  and "Edison effect," 98-99, 100-01
  electromagnet in measurement of, 50-51
  induced, 61, 63-65, 70, 71
  in telephone, 82
  magnetism in relation to, 44, 59-61
  of one ampere, 33
  photoelectric, 116, 118
  primary, in transformer, 73, 74
  and resistance, 33-34
  secondary, in transformer, 73, 74
  as stream of electrons, 27-28

Cyclotron, 45

De Forest, Lee, 103
Dial telephone, 85
Diode, 102
Direct current, 65, 66, 102
Doorbell, electric, 46-47

Edison, Thomas, 83, 98, 99
"Edison effect," 99
Einstein, Albert, 116
Electric current, *see* Current
Electric light, first, 7
Electric motor, *see* Motor, electric
Electricity, likened to action of water, 28-29, 30, 31, 32, 33, 92-93, 94
  and magnetism, 42, 44, 58-61, 63-65
  origin of name, 6
Electromagnet(s), 45, 57, 68, 69, 70
  in "atom-smasher," 52
  in buzzer, 46-47
  currents measured by, 50-51
  as lifting devices, 51
  in motors, 52
  in signaling devices, 51
  in telegraph system, 47, 48
  in telephone, 81, 85
  invention of, 79
Electron beam, in television, 129, 130, 131, 132, 134-35
Electron gun, in television, 129, 135-36
Electron tubes, 98-105
Electronic calculating machine, 125
Electrons, 15, 16, 29
  in barrier-layer photocell, 122
  frequency of vibration of, 96
  in heated filament of bulb, 100-01
  and light, 116*ff.*

Index

allabout
books